documentary photography

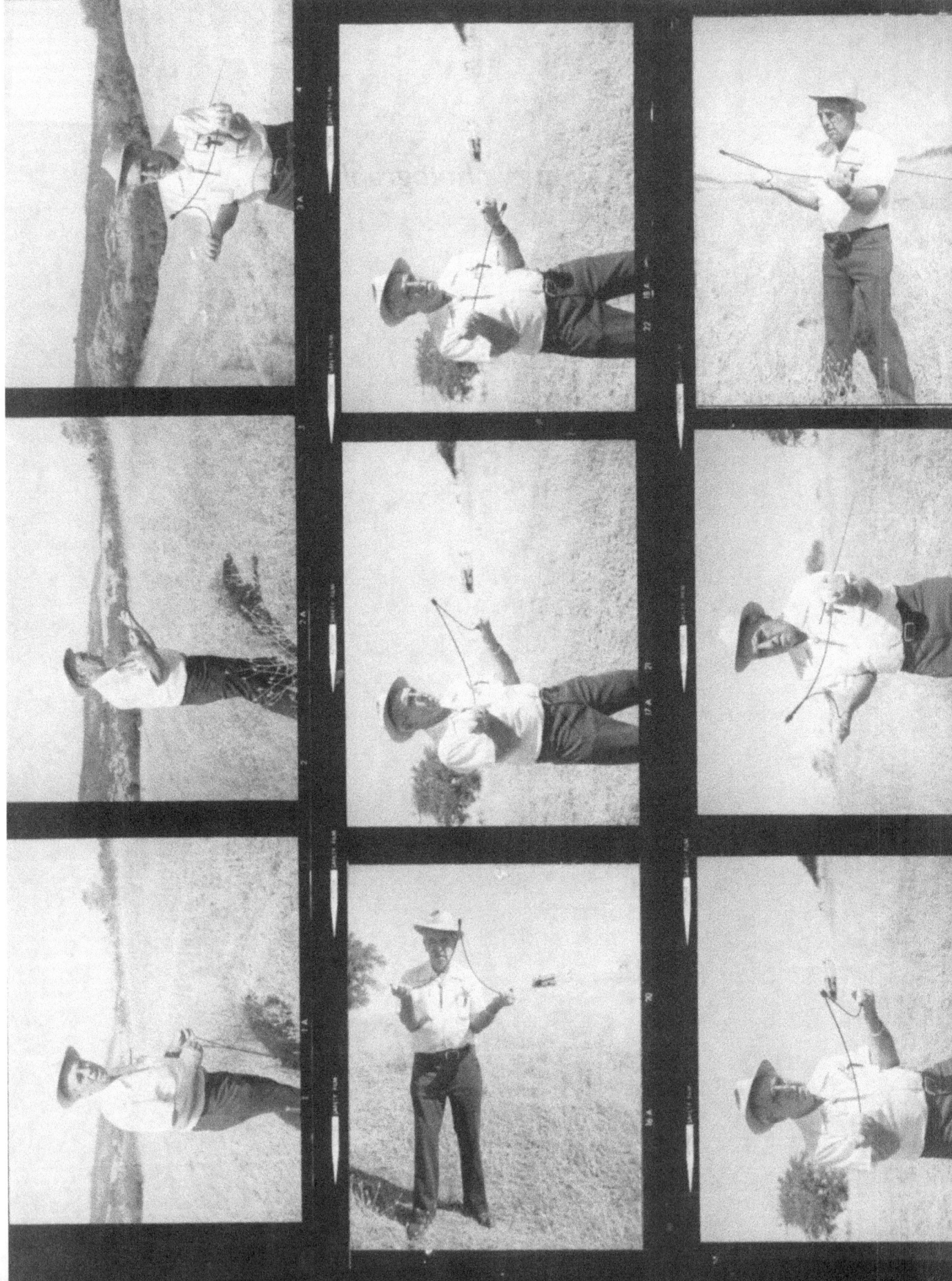

documentary photography

a personal view by bill owens

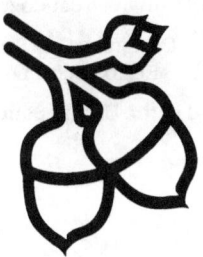

Addison House, Publishers
Danbury, New Hampshire

ISBN 978-0-9968277-6-8
Library of Congress catalogue no.: 78-57681

Design by Guy Russell
Editor, Scott Lowe

Printed in the United States of America

contents

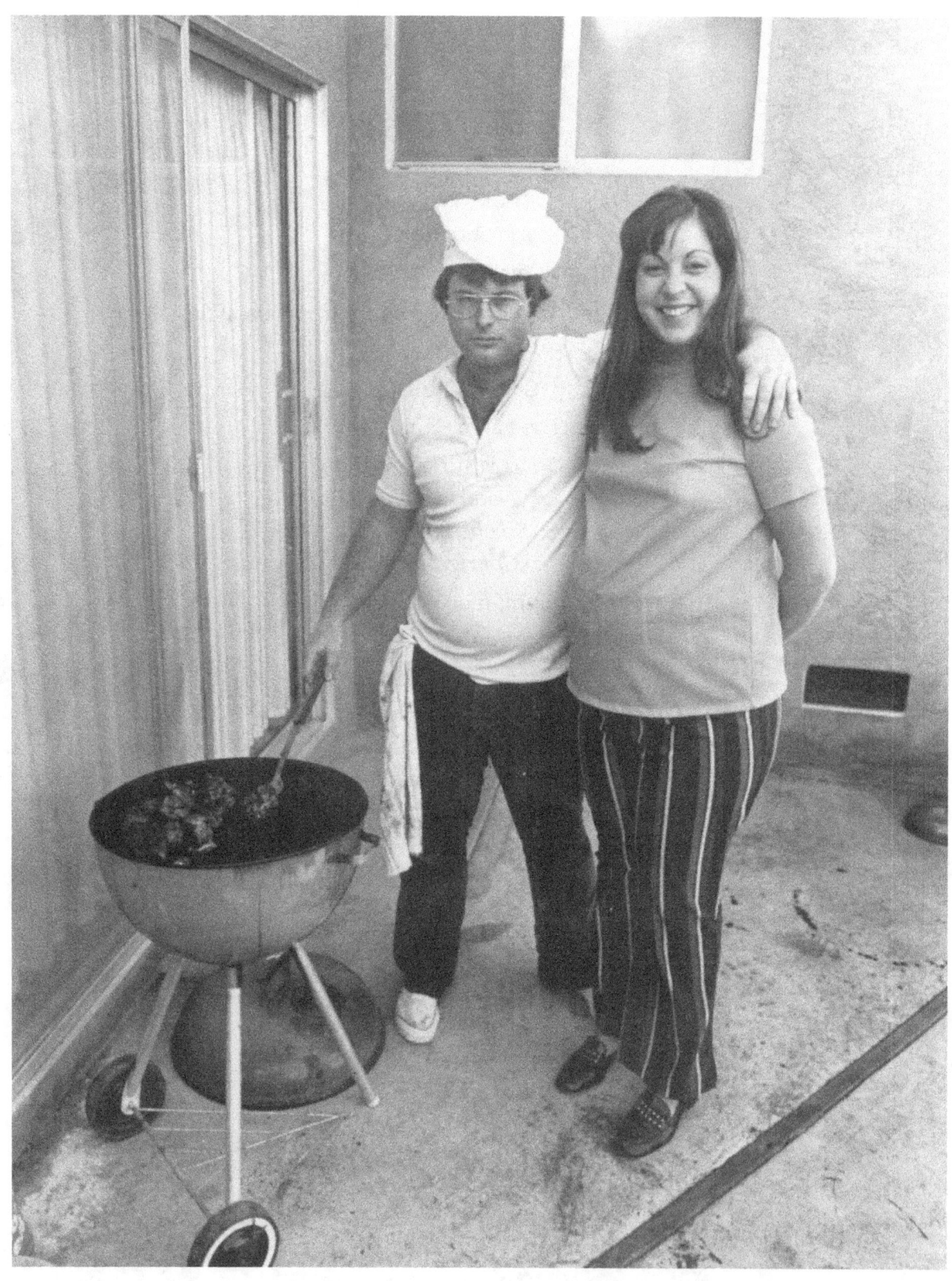

introduction

This book is my attempt to fill the void of information between the student of photography and the professional photographer. I'm addressing myself to the serious photographer who wants to know something about documentary photography as a profession, how to go about getting grants, and the factors involved in publishing a book.

I assume the people who read this book have a grasp of the basics, can load and shoot a 35mm camera, develop film and make photographic prints. If not, there are dozens of excellent how-to books that will teach you these things.

It takes years of patience, hard work, and self-criticism to develop a photographic style and learn the social and business aspects of photography. I hope this book contains some useful information about the documentary photographer's hardware, large cameras, strobe lighting, as well as why the quality of the photographic image is so critical to the documentary photograph.

Photography resembles sex: reading and talking about it is great, but doing it counts. Get out there and do it.

```
┌─────────────────────────────────────────────┐
│                                               │
│   DATE _____                       │
│                                               │
│              PHOTO  RELEASE                   │
│                                               │
│   I HEREBY GIVE BILL OWENS PERMISSION TO USE  │
│   MY PHOTOGRAPH, OR PHOTO OF MY PLACE OF      │
│   BUSINESS AND TO PUBLISH THE SAME WITHOUT IN-│
│   CURRING ANY DEBTS, LIABILITY TO ME (OR BILL │
│   OWENS) OF ANY KIND WHATSOEVER.              │
│                                               │
│   NAME: _____ │
│                                               │
│   ADDRESS: _____ │
│                                               │
└─────────────────────────────────────────────┘
```

getting started

Each year thousands of people buy cameras and take photography courses and workshops. Many of them believe that if they could only get a photograph in *Time* or *Newsweek* or perhaps an assignment for *People* they would have it made—or at least have made significant inroads in getting their careers off the ground. Others feel there is no way to break into photojournalism, that it is basically a closed profession. Both of these statements have their proponents. Even so, both these statements are untrue.

The real problem is this: how can a beginning photographer get started in this fascinating, if difficult, profession? How does one get the necessary experience so that one's photographic skills can grow from that of an amateur to that of a professional?

A point that I will make several times, and which must always be kept in mind, is that in photography, experience counts. The only way to learn it is to do it. One needs to make all the photographic mistakes—in the streets, in the darkroom and in selling your photographs. The mistakes are a necessary part of learning to "do" photography professionally.

My own particular experiences in learning to be a photojournalist, working on various projects and finally getting published will, I hope, be valuable for others intent on the same goals.

In March 1968, *Life* magazine published my photograph of a student riot at San Francisco State College. It was my first nationally published photograph, and from that moment on, I felt I was going to become a famous photojournalist. I could see it all: I would be on the staff of *Life* magazine; I would travel, have interesting assignments, and not the least of it, make a lot of money. However, two years later *Life* went out of business.

While I was a student at San Francisco State, I drove a taxi at night and worked as a photographer on the college newspaper. I also took photo art courses and studied visual anthropology. (There is nothing wrong with such studies as long as one realizes that they will contribute little or nothing toward the *real* requirements of a working photojournalist.)

The *best* place to get photographic experience is on a college newspaper. It's a real job! Assignments are given, and fulfilling those assignments is the quickest way to develop professional photographic skills. It is a good place to learn editorial needs and meet deadlines, as well as to accumulate tear sheets (printed samples of one's work) to show when applying for a more professional job. And when working for a college newspaper or even for one of the "underground papers," one learns how to cope and adjust to ever-changing demands.

Going to college and working for a college newspaper in the late Sixties often meant covering and confronting violence. While covering a student riot in 1968, I was mugged and managed to get my ribs kicked in. For all my trouble, those photos only made the San Francisco newspapers.

But I also made hundreds of dollars photographing student anti-war riots and their attendant violence. The photograph of a Hell's Angel beating someone was taken at the Rolling Stones Altamont concert. This particular photograph earned me quite a bit of money from newspapers and magazines across the country whose circulations thrive on images of violence and death.

Each year prizes are given to photographers who were at the right disaster at the right time: a shot of someone falling to his death, or, better yet, a photograph of someone holding a gun on a hostage, and being blasted at by the cops. Examine the book *Moments* and notice that many of the Pulitzer prize winning photos are of death scenes. Very few awards are given to serious photojournalists who make statements about our society. My photographic statements in *Suburbia* hopefully will stand the test of time because they reflect our times in a different way—a more humane way. My photographs of violence are not a source of personal pride.

So, with my tear sheets from the college newspaper, I spent four months looking for a job. If the opportunity came to work for *Life,* I was going to need practical experience—other than just covering riots.

I figured newspaper photography was the closest thing I could find to *Life* magazine. Finally, I got an interview at the *Independent* in Livermore, California. Happily, I was offered, and accepted, the job. I planned to stay one year and ended up staying eleven. I am still in Livermore today!

Once one graduates from a college newspaper, the best place to get a start is the small town or suburban newspaper. These papers are very often termed "throwaways." Basically they carry supermarket advertisements and the like, but they also have an editorial department and use photographers. As a small town photographer I was able to photograph for every section in the paper—editorials, women's pages, sports, features and advertising. It was an experience much more enriching than one can find with a large newspa-

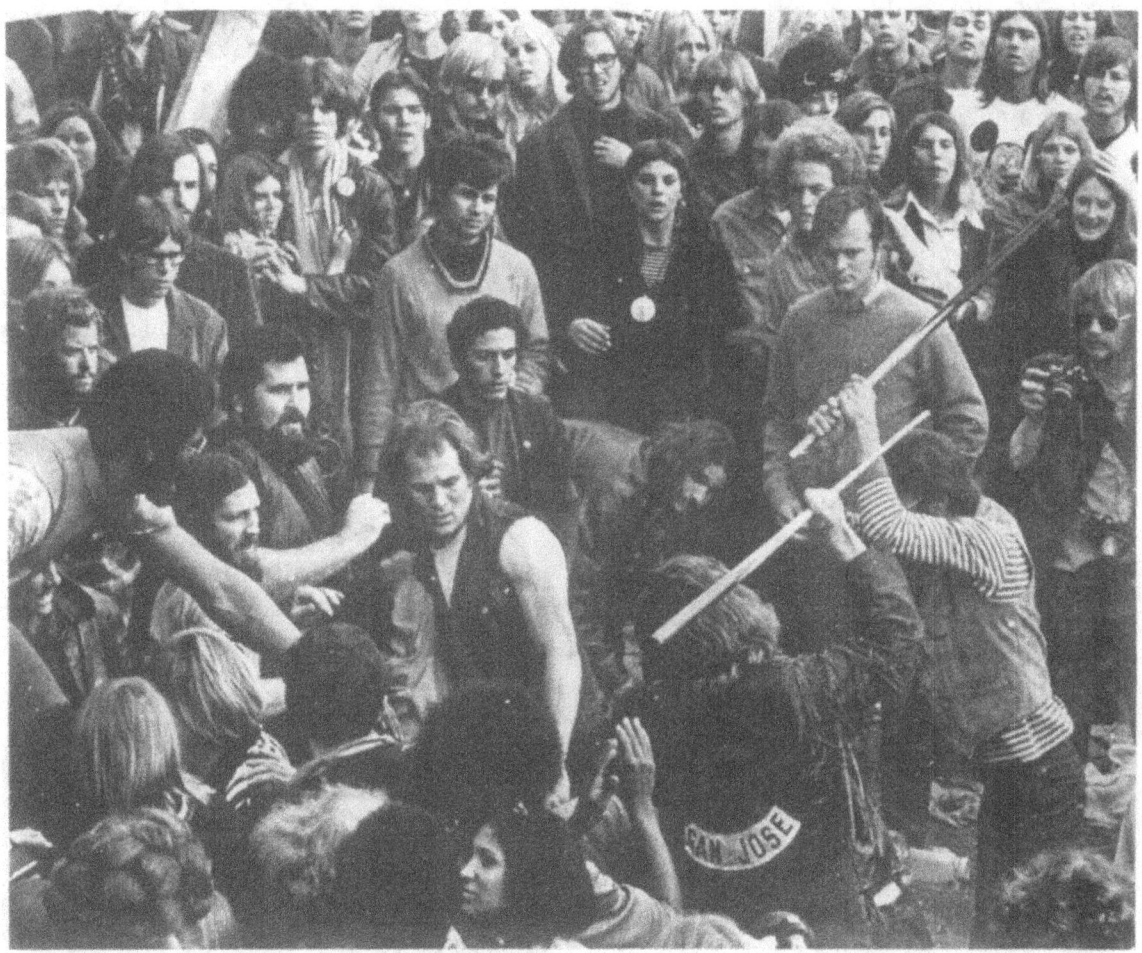

per. I did from seven to ten assignments a day; while on a large newspaper one seldom does more than two assignments daily.

For beginning photographers, I would recommend not trying to get a job with a large daily newspaper. They have unions for job protection and rigid methods of promotion. (Top paid news photographers now earn about $600.00 a week.) There are many things wrong with the large urban newspaper. The major obstacle for beginners, women especially, is that photographers who have a job at union scale never leave those jobs. Openings occur only when someone dies or retires, and neither happens very often. (The average age on large newspapers is usually about fifty.) The ranks of photographers on these papers include few women. Also, large newspapers are not creative places to work.

Editors for large newspapers and magazines often have fixed ideas and preconceptions about the acquisition and use of photographs. They give the assignments, crop the photographs and write the captions. And of course it is usually the case that good photographs get cropped or played down. With few exceptions, newspapers seldom print photographs correctly—and by correctly I mean "full frame."

And finally, working forty hours a week for a large newspaper leaves one with little time to develop one's own ideas or picture stories. A news photographer can become so busy that he has no time to do *photography*.

If one wants to do serious freelance work, then one must move to New York City or Los Angeles. Otherwise starvation will arrive before the bills are paid. There are only a handful of photographers who make a living by doing photojournalism exclusively. Most successful photographers do commercial work as well so they can choose their own assignments. Many end up doing commercial work for the money alone and never manage to develop a personal style or come to understand the importance of the photographic image.

So, if one is already in a large metropolitan area, here are a few hints in getting started. Every large city has numerous publications that use photographs to illustrate articles—for example, the Sunday magazine, city magazines and church magazines. Another good place to start is with the in-house magazines published by oil companies and other large industries. There are many of these types of magazines. Most have a low day rate (below $200.00), but they give out a great deal of work to freelancers.

Before approaching a particular magazine, study it to see what type of photographs it uses. If the magazine uses only black and white images, don't

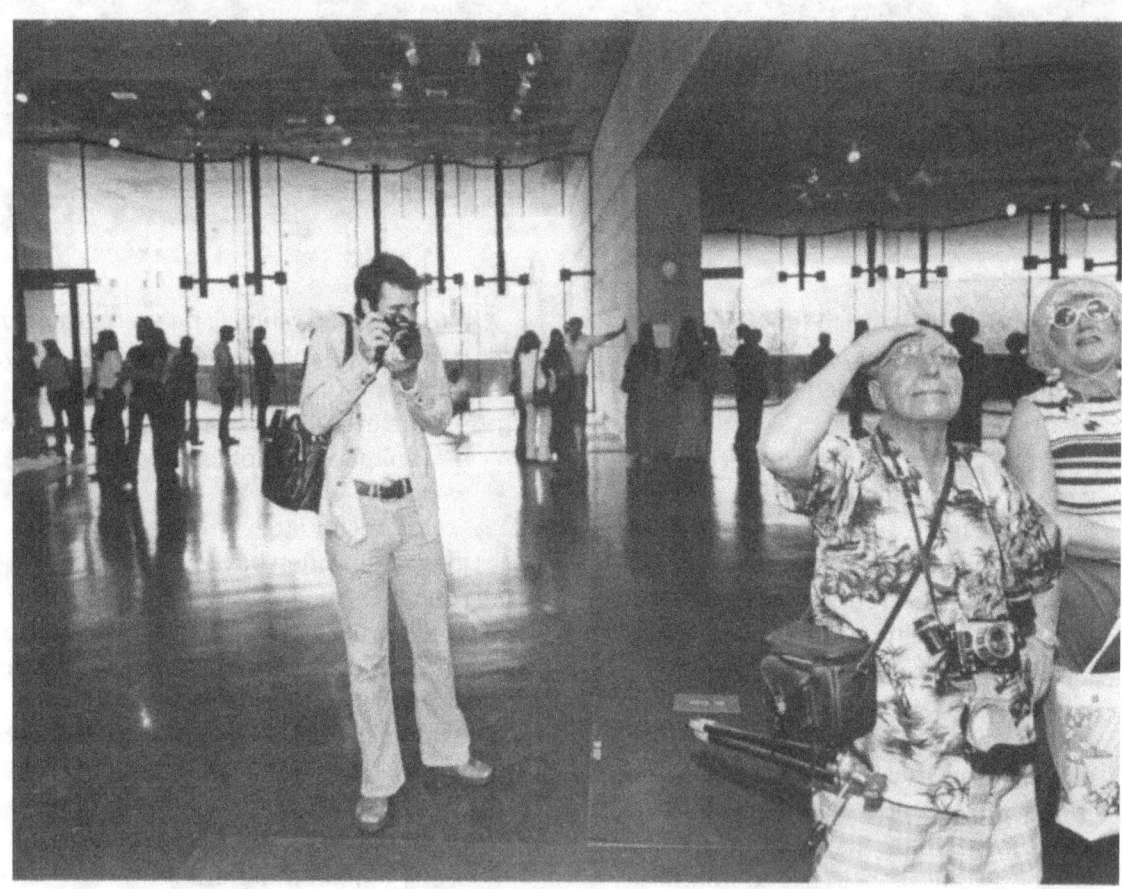

bother to bring color slides. It is up to you to come up with photographic ideas and stories the magazine might be able to use. When calling on an editor, show a *short* portfolio and include any work you have had published. Don't expect to be given an assignment immediately. Such magazines usually have photographers who work for them on a regular basis. Instead, shoot a carefully-prepared essay on speculation and try to sell it to them.

The successful photographer knows how to sell his work and himself, which brings us to another important point. Being a photographer requires one to be aggressive and persistent. I know of many mediocre photographers who work steadily simply because they can sell themselves. If possible, get acquainted with the magazine's assistant art director or the editor's secretary. Oddly enough, I've had many things published because a secretary liked my work!

And finally, make friends with other photographers and writers and share your information with them. They can help you understand how magazines work and how best to approach editors. In comparing it with other professions, photography has a very high rate of failure and dropout. It's a tough business, and sharing information is an important part of getting the work you want.

But to return to the second stage of one's growth as a photojournalist. It is good to know that some excellent photojournalism is being done for small town newspapers. They are the source of what may be the best jobs in photography today. There one has the freedom to use good photography and develop one's talents. If one can take a good picture of Little League baseball teams in action, then one can equally well take good pictures of the Oakland A's or the Cincinnati Reds!

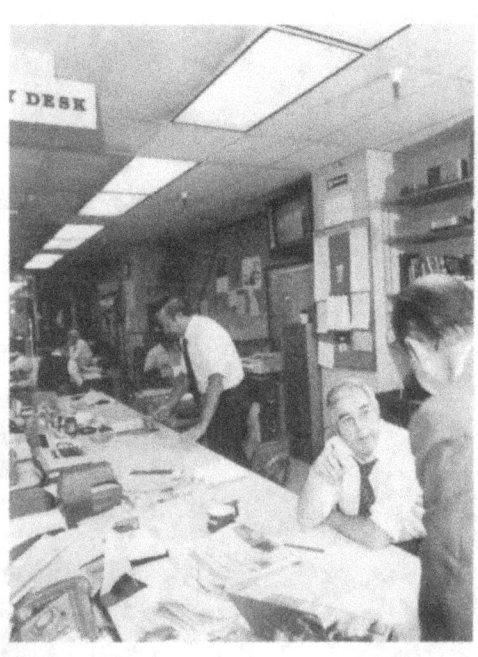

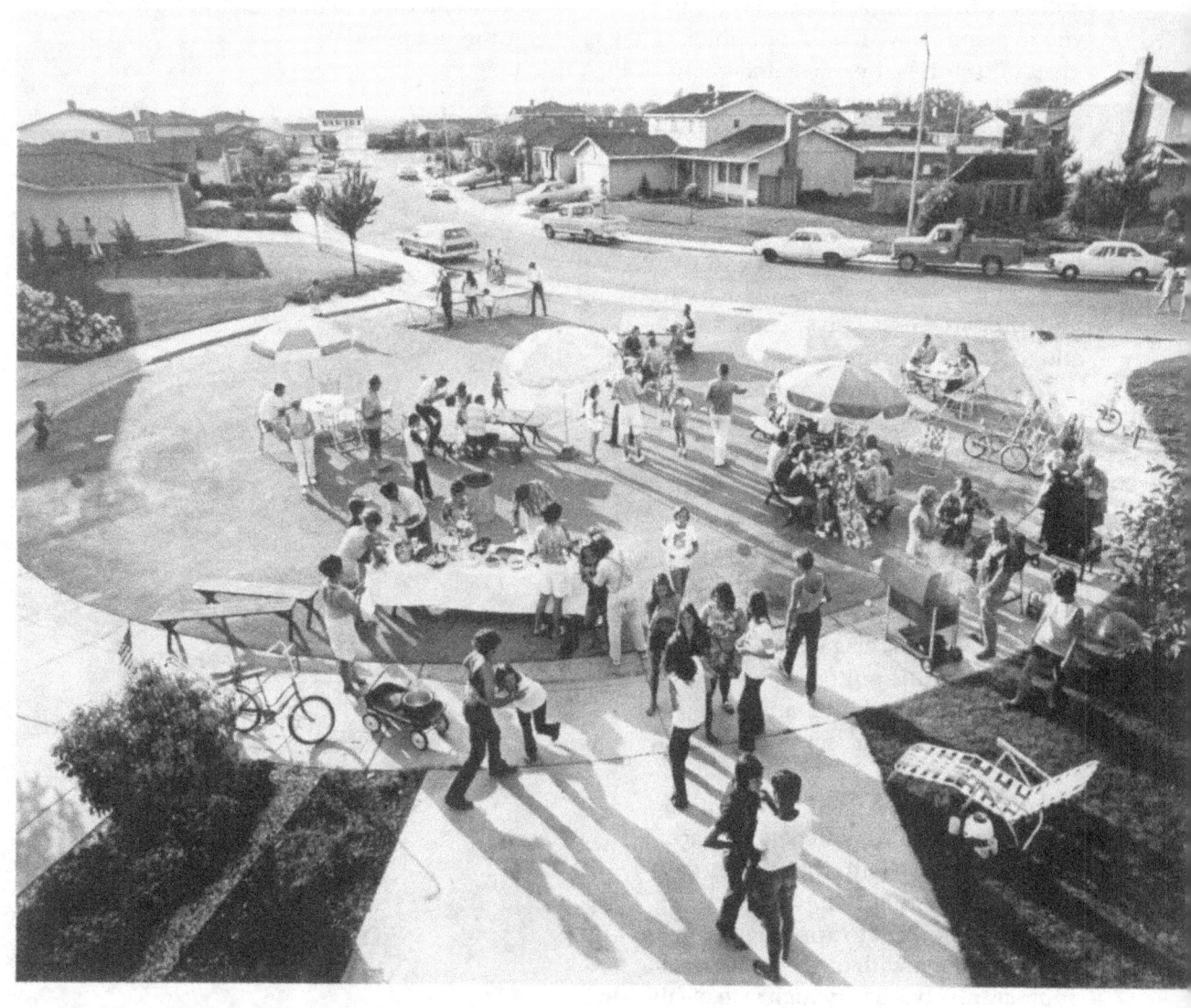

getting published:
Suburbia
and other
improbabilities

The suburbs of Livermore, California were something of a shock to me. Everyone there lives "the good life," which means having attractive homes, high paying jobs, swimming pools and shiny cars. I decided to do a documentary project on the suburbs—a visual/anthropological view of America.

When I started working on *Suburbia* in 1970 (my original title was *Instant America* because I felt then that the word "suburbia" had negative connotations), I didn't know any museum directors. Those I approached with the idea of doing such a documentary or having an exhibit on the subject weren't particularly interested. But I continued to ask various sources how I could get some money so that I could start on the project. After a year of showing my portfolio and talking with college professors, museum curators and staff, magazine editors and other photographers who had received grants, I finally found a businessman who was interested in helping me with the project. He gave me $2,000 as a "grant," in exchange for a set of prints. I felt he could see the importance of the *Suburbia* project from my portfolio and the statement of work plans. My portfolio consisted of fifty prints—and that was only the barest tip of the iceberg in the amount of work that would be done for this documentary. Only three of the original photographs from that portfolio are in *Suburbia.*

I feel the best way to start a documentary project is to give yourself a $500 grant. Use this money for film and printing, and spend one day a week for a year working on the project. Be assured that after a year you will have an interesting, and, hopefully, fine body of work.

An excellent documentary project to

undertake, and I feel an important one as well, is to photograph the city where you live. You needn't take on your home town as Atget took on Paris and its environs in the early 1900's, but he had the right idea. He knew the Paris of his time was rapidly fading, so he photographed its historic buildings, its fountains, trees, shops and streets and of course, its people. I approached the City Council of Livermore asking for $500 to take fifty photographs of buildings of historical importance to the city. This was the beginning of *Suburbia*.

It took several months of footwork, politics and phoning everyone of importance to get the money approved by the city. Then with the help of the City Beautification Committee, I selected thirty-five historical buildings and fifteen modern buildings. The last fifteen were schools, churches, banks and the typical tract home.

After the buildings were selected, I was able to photograph the project in three weekends. I made the prints myself from 2 1/4 negatives and managed to make $400 profit for my creative effort. But more importantly, there is now a photographic record (archival prints) of the fifty most important buildings in Livermore, California. These photographs are in the files of the city library.

With changes taking place so rapidly in this country, I feel that every city in America should hire photographers to make coherent and intelligent documentary records of the city's architecture, its general ambiance and its inhabitants at work and at play.

It is important to set a time limit on doing a documentary project. It makes one pull the project together and fill in the gaps—the photographs you always wanted to do but never did! In my own case it meant working day and night photographing everything from a Tupperware party to a family watching television. These events often don't happen on Saturdays between the hours of nine to five. Towards the end of my self-allotted time on the *Suburbia* project, I worked every weekend and Mondays, and, of course, on holidays, when people are doing what they like to do most. The more situations one gets into, the better one's chances to come up with some excellent images.

I visited some families six to ten times before I found *the* interesting photograph. With others I spent only ten minutes before I came up with a suitable photograph.

Working on your own time is important because as you shoot you will gradually get an intimate sense for the project. You will also find out if it's something you really want to do. After shooting about fifty rolls of film, examination of your work will help you to

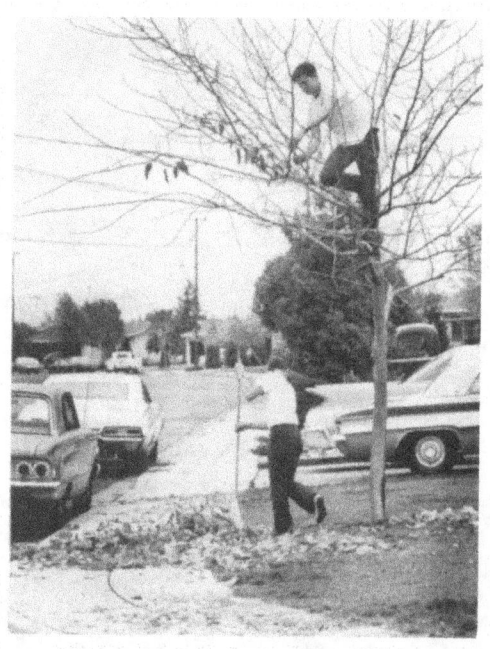

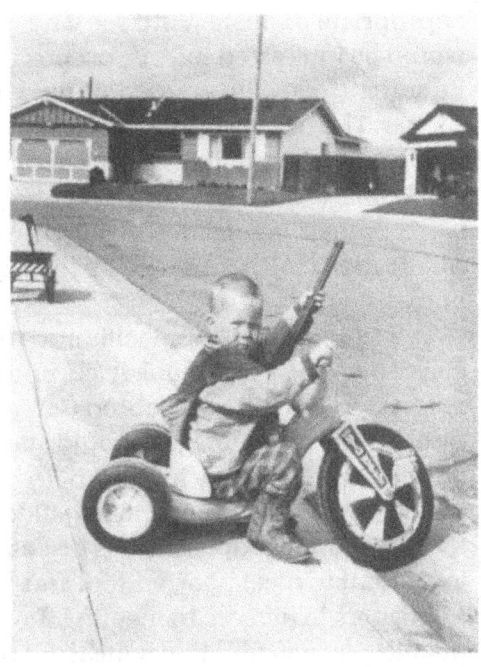

develop specific ideas for the "statement of work plans." And of course one can then use the resulting portfolio to show others what the documentary project is all about.

It may be interesting to contrast my situation while shooting *Suburbia* with that of a *National Geographic* staff photographer. At *National Geographic* an assignment can last up to two years. A major story will cost from $35,000 to $75,000. The photographer will probably shoot more than 500 rolls of color film, and if the story runs thirty-two photographs, each photograph will have cost approximately $2,700!

I didn't have seven days a week and a virtually unlimited budget to produce *Suburbia*. The book contains 128 images, and I produced the book for $3,600. The important difference is that I was not an outsider coming in from a big magazine, shooting hundreds of rolls of film and departing, never to see

those people again—I had a relationship with the people who were my subjects, and I retained complete control over the project. I could photograph what interested me, without editors telling me what I had missed and instructing me to go back and do it again. I was truly interested in how the middle class lived and felt about themselves. And I felt that if people could become aware of their life styles in some way, and have a better appreciation of it, they could change it for the better. I could hardly believe that an American family might spend as much as $350 a year on the care and feeding of the family pet!

To emphasize a point made earlier, my job as a newspaper photographer opened up the community for me. I had access to everyone from civic leaders and business people to housewives and mothers. Many of these people needed publicity photographs taken for the newspaper. And it was largely through the newspaper that I was able to make friends with many others who were later to become photographic subjects for my book projects. At some point I even ran classified ads in the paper saying, "I am working on a photographic project about suburbia. I would like to photograph your home, your children, pets, or whatever." Many people phoned and invited me into their homes, where I took some of the best photographs in the book.

I could have earned a great deal of money over the last eight years as a commercial photographer or in a related profession. But I thought it more important to produce an honest documentary record of how my family and friends live.

When I had finally finished the project, I selected 500 prints. It was at this point that I went looking for a publisher. I showed the prints that were to be *Suburbia* to Straight Arrow Books, and they agreed to publish it. But they didn't exactly plan to subsidize me for the rest of my life.

The arrangement with Straight Arrow Books was for a $1500 advance and 6% royalty payment. It is important to understand that an advance is an advance on royalties; that is, once sales of my book earned $1500 in royalties, *then* I would begin to receive royalty payments. At first I was a little upset about this arrangement. At that rate I would make only 35¢ per copy, thus not even breaking even on the project. (The prints alone had cost me approximately $2,000.) But when I phoned another photographer, I learned from him that $1500 advance and 6% royalty rate is standard for a book by an unknown photographer. It became clear that having *Suburbia* published was not going to make me rich and famous. As it turned out, I had to continue as a small town newspaper photographer for six more years and publish two more books *Our Kind of People and Working (I Do It For The Money)* before I could free myself enough to work as a freelance photographer. It is interesting to note that even with three books out, the most I would receive in a year would be $2,000 in royalties.

Even though a great deal of money is not in the offing, it is still of prime importance for a photographer to be published. Having a book published opens the doors for other opportunities—teaching, workshops, lectures, grants and establishing one's reputation.

If you have developed an idea for a book and feel you are on to something important, my advice is to phone an appropriate publisher and see if he would be interested in your proposal. Be sure to follow up your enquiries with a letter. The major source books for information on publishers are *Literary Marketplace* and *Photography Marketplace,* both of which are R. R. Bowker publications. All libraries carry these books.

The letter should be specific and discuss how you see the book itself, not so much the visual theory behind the photographs. The images should stand on their own. It is very important to write concise letters and clearly-stated, thorough book proposals. It is just as important to meet book editors and publishers in person. In meeting these people, you will find that a measure of tact and some comprehension of the publishing process will go a long way toward furthering your cause.

Once a publisher has the project in hand, he will analyze the probable production costs and possible markets for the book. Book publishers are understandably leery of publishing most photographic books because they are expensive to produce and slow to sell.

The economics of it are fairly straightforward: if you have a book published and the retail price is $10.00, you will be lucky to make 80¢ per copy (8% of retail price). Where does all the money go, you ask? Well, the publisher sells your book to the bookstore for about 46% of the retail price. This percentage varies from publisher to publisher. Out of the money remaining, the publisher will have to invest most of it in the following ways: a sizable portion per book will go for paper, printing, binding and design. Photographic books are very expensive to produce. Then the author would receive his allotment, but portions of the remaining money must still go to salesmen, publicity services and storage and shipping of the books. This leaves the publisher with a grand total of about 10% profit, if that. The profit is not immediate either, because it takes a long time (a year or more in most cases) to sell out the first printing of a photographic book.

On the first printing the publisher makes less money than the author. The difference is that the publisher has invested thousands of dollars to print a few thousand copies of the book. If the book sells the entire first printing, the publisher has probably gotten back his investment but has failed to make a profit. On subsequent printings money can be made because the initial costs of development, design and the making of negatives or color separations has been eliminated.

It only makes sense then to assume that a photographic book publisher won't take on a book project unless he is fairly certain that it will at least break even. Naturally, the publisher hopes to make money from the book, but the statistics are against him. Most photographic books fail to sell the number of copies necessary to pay for themselves, and many of them fail to earn back their production cost.

Photographic books fall into three general categories. The first is the *monograph*. This is the one that is so risky to publish and is responsible for the abysmal figures I quoted above. It is difficult to make money on this type of book because of the extreme high costs of fine printing and production and because of the difficulty of selling a fine art or purely photographic book to the public. The principal market for this sort of book is the photographic community itself, which is not noted for its purchasing power. Out of fifty monographs published in a year, fewer than ten will do more than merely pay for themselves, and very few of those will be reprinted. Many never even sell out the first printing. Unless the photographer is extremely well-known, or the subject particularly topical, such books inevitably encounter a very limited buying public.

The second type of photographic book is the *in-house book*. These are usually assigned by the editor or the publisher and sold by various means— direct mail, consignment, etc. These can be "how-to" books or fine quality books as produced by *Time-Life, National Geographic, Addison House, New York Graphics*, etc. Books produced on this basis have a better chance of selling well, but still, the investment is enormous. The in-house type of book can also include scholarly books of various sorts. These could range from books on contemporary photographic criticism to those on aspects of the history of photography. In this case the photographs are more illustrative and supportive of text than presented as images for their own sake.

The final category of photographic books is *illustrated trade books*. This sort of book often incorporates a percentage of color reproductions along with black and white photos. The variations on this kind of book are virtually infinite. Photographers *and* illustrators can often be involved in a project of this type. Illustrated trade books cover such topics as nature, building, movies, film making, science fiction or whatever currently holds the public interest. Naturally, this type of book has tremendous sales potential because of mass market appeal and a traditional up-beat view of the world. These are the books that keep the publishing industry and photographers alive and well.

One can begin to see then the diversity of the publishing world and the demand for originality and quality on the part of an aspiring photographer. A photographer can't produce one book like the *Thorn Birds* or one movie like *Star Wars* and suddenly find himself (or herself) rich and famous overnight. That *one* book can't make you. There are no sudden stars in photography. It takes years of hard work and learning the craft to achieve success. And one successful book doesn't mean a publisher will sign you for a second book automatically. Each book has to stand on its own merit. The simple truth is that a photographic book rarely sells 50,000 copies, and one isn't likely to see such a book on the *New York Times* Best Seller List.

Suburbia was a good project—not only was it satisfying for me, but the book got rave reviews. Even the *New York Times* liked it. "Well," I thought, "now I will become famous." (Everyone gets his turn.) *Time, Newsweek* and even *People* would be calling to send me to some exotic location on assignment. Perhaps *National Geographic* would like my book. . . .

Nothing happened. One year passed without the pleasure of that special phone call. I started work on my second book, *Our Kind of People,* published two years later. It also got excellent reviews, and still the phone didn't ring. But the dream was still there: numerous assignments, travel, and photographing all kinds of interesting people and events. That was while I still thought editors bought photographic books.

In the spring of 1976 the phone finally *did* ring. I had published three books and waited seven years for that phone call. It was *Newsweek.* They wanted to know if I would be "interested in a photographic assignment"! I was to photograph the "Sun Belt Series" for the Fourth of July Bicentennial issue of the magazine. It was my dream assignment—three weeks of travel, fascinating people and $2,000 for my creative efforts! Naturally I purchased a used Mercedes-Benz 220 Diesel. Hoo boy!

With the help of Bank Americard, I began my assignment by flying off to Arizona. I became very familiar with Budget-Rent-A-Car and Holiday Inn. I photographed tourists in their campers in the middle of the desert, Zuni pueblos, and even a hippie commune in Taos, New Mexico.

One week later, back in California, I received a call from the senior editor at *Newsweek.* With great tact he said, "Listen, what I'm about to say may bore you, but if we don't get this straight, *you* are going to be in deep trouble. America isn't all dirt roads and flat expanse. We need you to show some of the good life, like you do in your books. Show us people swimming, vacationing, shopping, carousing and generally having a good time. Give us more of the *cities* in the 'Sun Belt.'" So within two hours I was flying to Houston and then from there to Orlando. There is a crazy pressure when you have to photograph all of Houston, Texas or Phoenix, Arizona in three days. What can really be said or shown about a city in three days? Only the Chamber of Commerce's view of the city. If you are lucky, you might come up with some pretty post card photographs.

Some fifty rolls of film and two weeks later, totally exhausted, I was back in California. On the Fourth of July the *Newsweek* article appeared, and five pages of my photographs were displayed, showing the "Sun Belt States."

But my hopes were smashed—the photographs were cropped. In a photograph of a room full of people dancing, I preferred the overview. But, typically, the editors wanted close-up photographs of attractive women. They cropped the photograph and just showed the good-looking women! On such assignments, one has to do what the editors require. You give the editors what they want: they have final control over the fate of your photographs. It's a difficult situation. Everyone liked the photo essay but me. Cropping the photos negated my style, and thus the essay lacked my photographic "look." I was homogenized and reduced to fit *Newsweek's* style.

Newsweek must have liked the photo essay because three weeks later they sent me to Kansas City to document the 1976 Presidential convention. In one week I shot another fifty rolls of film. But this photo essay looked much better than the first: they ran the photos full frame.

But when I got back to California I was a physical wreck and couldn't work for three weeks. The dream of being a photojournalist is crazy! It isn't fun to shoot fifty rolls of film as fast as you can shoot it and never even see what you got. Nor is it fun to stay in the ubiquitous Holiday Inn, eat plastic food and sleep with the air conditioner on. And to top it off, most of the people I had met were not particularly interesting. After three weeks on the road, my kids didn't recognize me and my wife was understandably hostile because I had been having "fun" while she had to stay home with the kids.

So, to return to an earlier theme, the only real photojournalism is produced while working for a small town newspaper where one has the freedom to select the best photographs. One might have to complete six to eight assignments a day, but there is a measure of freedom. There is a basic and important difference between doing a magazine story and creating a book. With the book, one has time to produce it in a proper fashion and the pressure of work comes from within. On assignments for a large circulation magazine or newspaper, one has to produce something eye-catching, and time works against you.

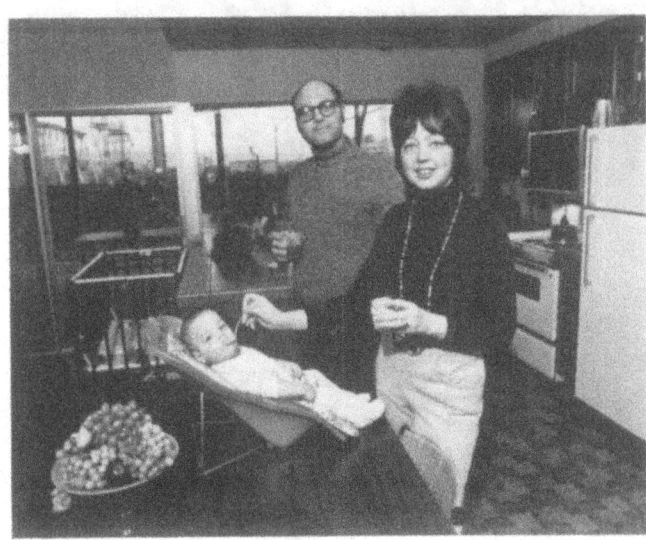

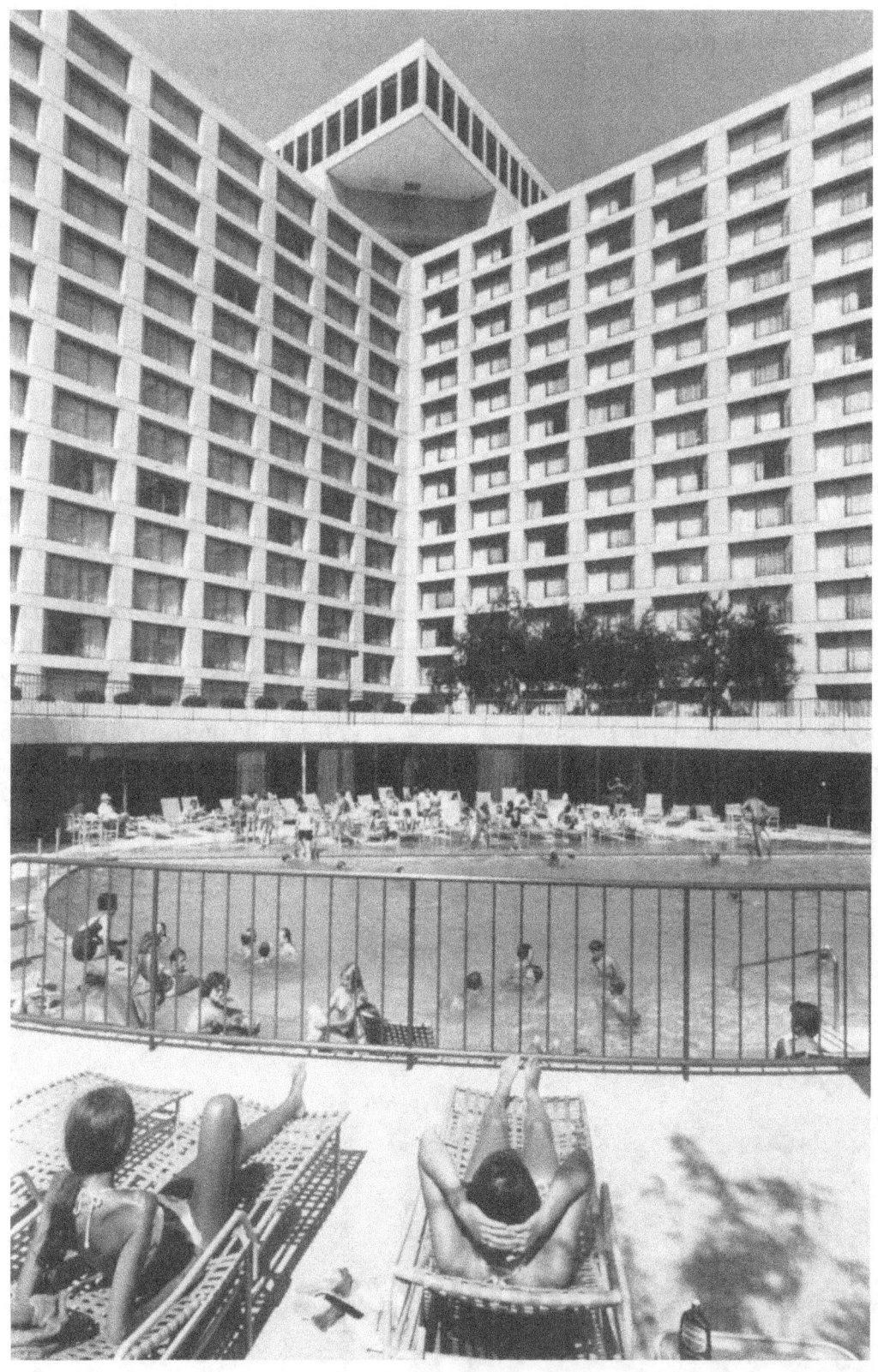

grants

Suburbia took a year to plan, a year to photograph and one more to get published. None of it would have been possible without the initial "grant" from my businessman friend. The photographic grant is at the very heart of doing a documentary project. The money allows one to buy time, equipment, film, and the room to operate. And receiving a grant is the outward symbol that one is doing something interesting. (At least it should be interesting to you. It may not prove interesting to an art museum director or a book publisher, but that's another matter.) Once *Suburbia* was published and had received critical acclaim (a significant qualification), the museum people became interested in having exhibits, and I received invitations to be part of group shows as well.

As I indicated earlier, the most practical way to start on a documentary project is to give yourself a $500 grant for the purchase of film and printing. The ideal situation is to receive one of the two major photographic grants given in this country. They are the National Endowment for the Arts (NEA) and the John Simon Guggenheim Fellowship.

The more accessible of the two grants is the NEA. This is because the grant is given to forty photographers selected from an average of (only!) three thousand applicants. Two even more important factors with regard to the NEA are that your work is judged solely on its merit and personal references are not required. Even so, prior to applying for this or any other major grant, it is best to spend several years working on your own and having at least two exhibitions of your work. Having an exhibition and getting your show reviewed in the newspaper is very important. The attention in the press can lead to articles in *Camera 35, Popular Photography* or other photographic periodicals. In order to be recognized as a photographic artist it is important (but not as critical as it used to be) to have photographs published in *Aperture* or *Camera* magazine.

If you do plan to submit an application to the National Endowment for the Arts or to the Guggenheim Foundation, I have two suggestions: the first is to make photographic prints that are absolutely perfect. Your portfolio must be consistent in both theme and point of view. The second suggestion concerns the "statement of work plan" for the Guggenheim grant, which may be even more important than the photographs themselves. One must write a concise statement elucidating the ideas behind the project and its goals. (It took me three months to write the proposal for *Suburbia*.) Photographers don't usually write about their creative efforts prior to taking a photograph. To get a Guggenheim grant, however, one must do just that—describe the project in advance of taking the photographs. In the final section of this book are my statements of work plans for *Suburbia*, *Our Kind of People* and *Working (I Do It For The Money)*. In each case I had photographic prints that strongly reinforced the grant statement. I received grants and managed to get published without having a family trust fund, a working wife or a high paying job. Over a period of seven years I have received $22,000 in grant money. But the books and the grants didn't support me: this money only brought film and supplies! These projects are labors of love, and the process of creating books has become part of my lifestyle.

The most difficult and prestigious grant is the John Simon Guggenheim Fellowship. Every year a maximum of seven photographers receive between $10,000 and $18,000 to work on individual projects. To receive a Guggenheim, one must present a beautiful set of photographs and a precise statement of work plans. In addition, and this is the really difficult part, one must have four personal references who will submit letters of support. The references that will make a difference are those from museum and photographic gallery directors—not those from other photographers, as many people think. The Guggenheim Foundation (which is separate from the Guggenheim Museum) wants to know what museum directors and photographic curators have to say about the applicant's work.

Exhibits, reviews and magazine articles about one's work give the exposure one needs to meet critics, curators, writers and college professors. These contacts are necessary to get the references one must have for a Guggenheim grant. Getting to know the "right" person can be important, but it is your photographs that really count. With the publication of *Suburbia* I was able to have museum and gallery exhibits, get photo essays from the book published in newspapers and magazines, and to win second place in the 1972 *Life* Magazine contest. This was possible because of the book itself, not because I knew anyone important in the photographic business or had a photographic agency representing me.

It is necessary to make trips to New York to meet magazine and book editors and publishers as well as other photographers. Contacts lead to photographic assignments and an enrichment of one's professional life. It is a variation of the old game—publish or perish. Visibility and recognition, as well as talent and drive, are keys to eventual success.

JOHN SIMON GUGGENHEIM MEMORIAL FOUNDATION

90 Park Avenue · New York, N.Y. 10016

APPLICATIONS and accompanying documents should reach the office of the Foundation not later than the date specified in our announcement.

Name in full (surname in capitals) **William Elmo OWENS**

Preferred mailing address **Yosemite Dr.   Livermore, California 94550**

Zip Code   Telephone **(415) 447-5943**

Home address (if other than above)

Zip Code   Telephone

Title of present position (include name of institution, if any)

News Photographer

State the specific field of scholarship or art in which your proposal lies

PHOTOGRAPHY

State concisely the title of your project **A photo study of group rituals and social behavior in suburbia**

State where you intend to carry out your proposed plan **California**

Specify the inclusive dates of the period for which you are requesting a Fellowship

Summer 1975 to Summer 1976

Place of birth **San Jose, California**   Date of birth **9-25-38**   Sex **M**

Citizenship **U.S.A.**   If not a native-born citizen, give date and place of naturalization:

Marital status **Married**   Number and ages of children **Two boys ages six and two**

Name and address of spouse or nearest kin **Janet Louise Owens   address same as above**

Social Security number (if U.S. citizen or resident) **549-50-0628**

Educational Summary	Name of Institution	Period of Study (*give dates*)	Degrees, Diplomas, Certificates (*give dates*)
Academic: Undergraduate	Chico State College	1957 to 1963	B.A. 1963
Graduate	San Francisco State	1967-68	
Other: (Artistic, Musical, etc. where pertinent)			

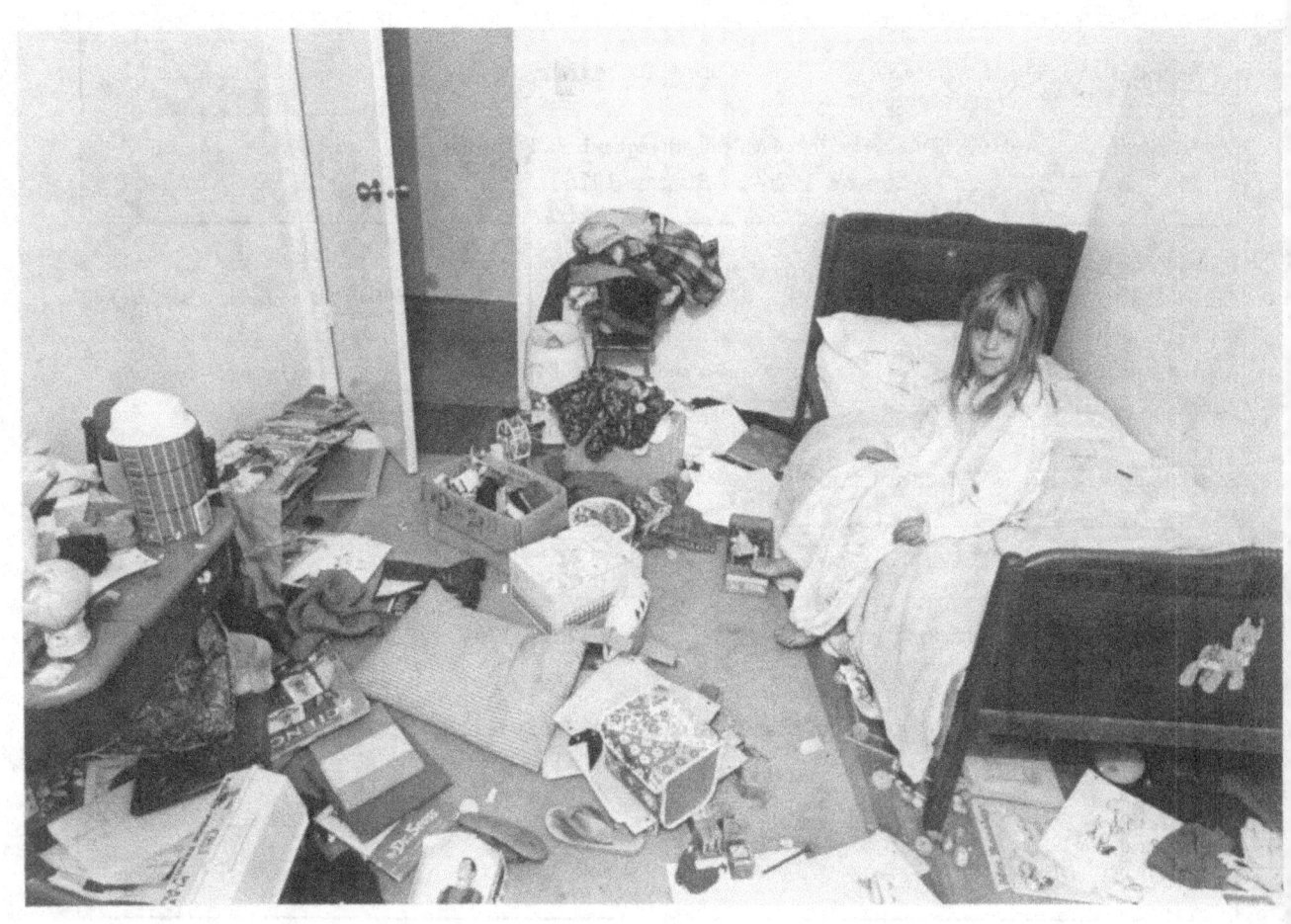

general rules

I have found that there are a few general rules which prove themselves very useful when on assignment. They are common sense items for the most part, but they only become so after they have been forgotten a few times! Keeping these rules in mind could save a lot of aggravation and grief in the future.

1. *Be familiar with your subject.* A photographer can usually do a much better job if he knows vital bits of information about the person or situation he is to photograph. If you are covering a topic you know little about, do some preliminary research to familiarize yourself with the subject. Having this information beforehand eliminates the need to ask unnecessary questions.

When dealing directly with individuals, try to establish a rapport with them. Once a certain ease is established, it is usually possible to do a better job photographing that subject, and the session then becomes a natural process. There are some photographers who rely on the "gift of gab" to avoid doing any preliminary homework. I wouldn't recommend this practice, however, as it can result in sloppy and unprofessional sessions.

Once on assignment, my suggestion is to shoot a few frames, stop and talk with the subject for a few minutes, and then change the location to shoot a few more frames. This keeps the session moving nicely, as well as serving to relax the subject.

Another point to keep in mind is that the camera itself can become an obstacle between photographer and subject. A simple way to overcome that is by hanging the camera over one's shoulder after shooting a roll of film and chatting informally with the subject. By alternately shooting and talking, the session will take on a natural rhythm.

There are times, of course, when you will need to have the subject do something in particular, such as looking directly into the camera. Directing your subject is much easier if there is a genuine rapport between the two of you.

2. *Watch professional photographers at work.* Professional photographers usually develop a strong sense of where to be and how best to react in any given situation. Because *viewpoint* counts for so much in documentary photography, half the battle is getting in the right place to get the shot you want. Notice which cameras and lenses professionals use in certain situations, what angles they shoot from and where they stand in relation to their subject.

You will notice that most professional photographers are extremely flexible. They can generally make rapid adjustments in either their methods or equipment to meet the needs of a given assignment.

3. *Photograph your subjects from more than one position.* Prior to shooting an assignment, consider what sort of information about the subject is essential. Then move in and out, varying the perspective and photographing from different angles and positions. This variation in position and distance adds to or subtracts information from the photograph. At a later time one can select which prints most effectively communicate who and what the subject is about—at least as much as can be communicated by images alone.

4. *Get the overview.* At any gathering, one should always take the trouble to get the overview. Record the number of people present. (Are there twenty or two hundred people at the wedding?)

An overview must show not only the participants, but also the setting in which the gathering takes place. Bring a

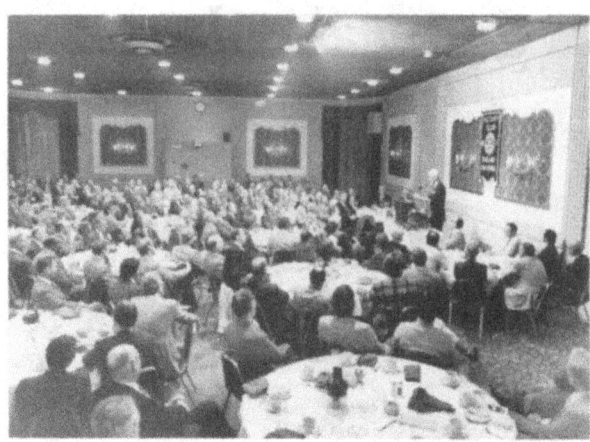

ladder, stand on a table, climb a tree, or do whatever it takes to get the large perspective. After the overview, one can record the details of the event. But remember that it isn't a good idea to get so involved in the event that you neglect the assignment—photograph first, drink later!

5. *Ask permission to take a photograph.* Unless it's absolutely essential to the assignment, don't catch people unawares when taking their photographs. Common courtesy is a factor here, but also many a photographer has been yelled at or even physically attacked for doing just that.

Cooperation is much more likely if you explain that you are a photographer on assignment. It may be necessary to promise them a print, but most people will understand immediately and gladly give permission to have their pictures taken.

Courtesy is just good business. Be friendly and thank your subjects for allowing you to photograph them. This policy can save time and complications if, at a later time, you need to have a photo release form signed.

6. *Dress appropriately.* An interesting characteristic about photographs is

that the one who took the photograph is usually not visible. But the photographer is often very visible during the process of taking his photographs. For this reason, it pays to look good and dress appropriately when on assignment. (If one is covering the opening of the Opera season, come in tails and top hat!) It's not really necessary to look like you just stepped out of the pages of *Gentlemen's Quarterly*, but one does need to fit in with the milieu in which one photographs, whatever that might be.

7. *Shoot a lot of film.* Don't hesitate to shoot two rolls of film (72 frames) on a subject. One must be either very lucky or a great photographer (or both) to get that right shot in only a few frames. On a good day, I can shoot three frames and know I've got the shot I want. But there are many more days when I'll shoot ten rolls of film and be fortunate to get anything at all worth printing.

Film is the least expensive item one must purchase (averaging about a nickel a shot). I shoot everything I can, because often it isn't possible to return and reshoot the event. Most assignments are one-shot affairs, so one must get it right the first time. It used to be that way for weddings as well, but nowadays there is a very good chance one will cover the same wedding again under slightly different circumstances!

8. *Always carry extra rolls of film.* It's a good idea to keep film on your person or in a small ice chest in the car. The very worst thing that can happen on assignment, short of losing one's camera and equipment, is to run out of film. It is surprising, really, how frugal or forgetful some photographers are about this vital piece of merchandise.

I've made all the mistakes a photographer can make, including this one. I once walked three miles through deep snow and bitter cold to an elevation of 12,000 feet, only to find that I had three color shots on one camera and two black and white shots on the other. My collection now sports only five photographs of the Bristle Cone pine trees!

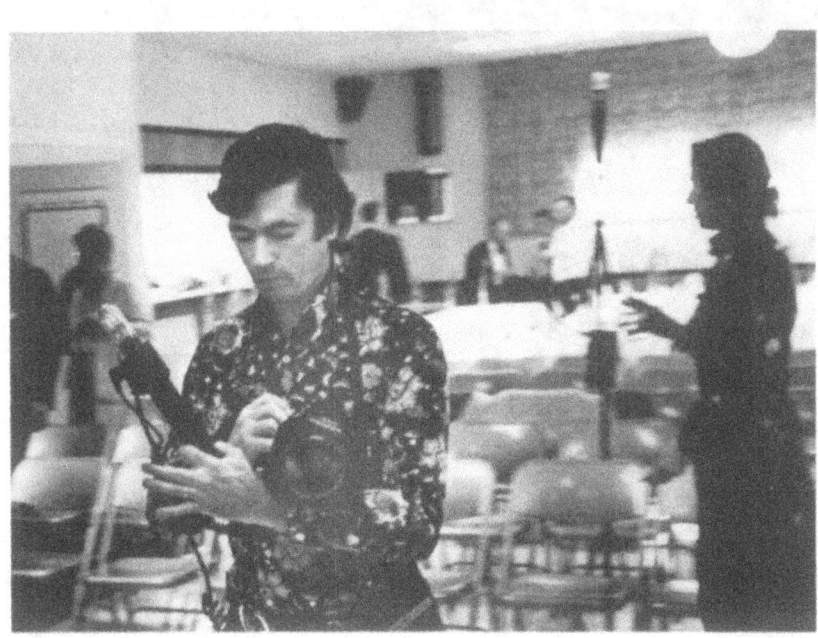

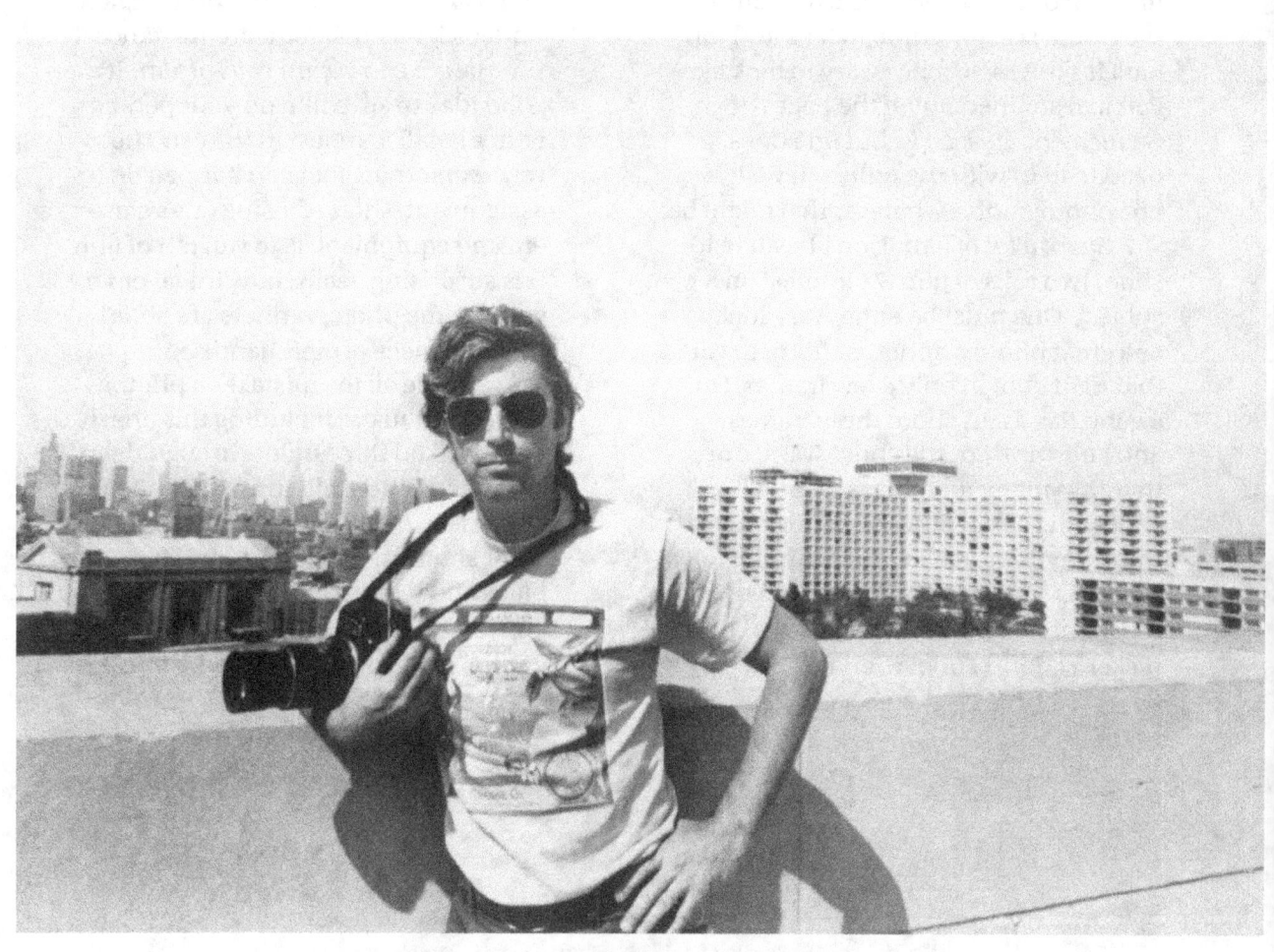

the large camera

The most popular photographic technique today is to use a 35mm camera, Tri-X film and natural light. Most photographers shoot for "composition." The negative is then printed to get the richest blacks possible. This technique was advocated by *Life* Magazine in the 50's and is still widely used today. I would like to reverse this process and make photographic prints which have rich middle greys and a minimum of blacks.

Another trend in photojournalism is the use of a motor drive on the 35mm camera, allowing the photographer to shoot many frames of a subject very quickly. My feeling about the widespread use of motor drive is that it serves two purposes: it makes it possible for Kodak to continue paying generous dividends to its stockholders and it also keeps photo editors busy screening endless trays of nearly identical transparencies. The use of the motor drive is based on the same principle as the shotgun. If you shoot long enough and fast enough, at least one outstanding photo is bound to result! I've done three documentary projects now which have culminated in published books, and I haven't needed a motor driven unit yet.

The photograph of the three women sitting around the table and chatting was taken on one of my first newspaper assignments. It was shot with a Nikon, using a 28mm (wide angle) lens and Tri-X film. As you can see, the photo is not very sharp, and because it's so contrasty, it is difficult to look at. I showed this print, as well as some of my other newspaper material, to Paul Glines, a photojournalist who works for the *San Francisco Examiner*. He suggested that, in order to achieve full-tone prints, I might try using a large format camera

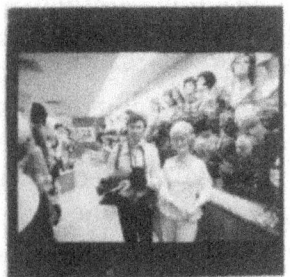

35MM

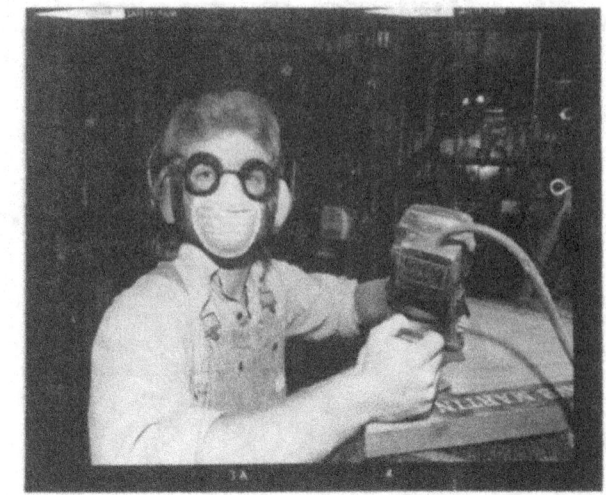

6x7

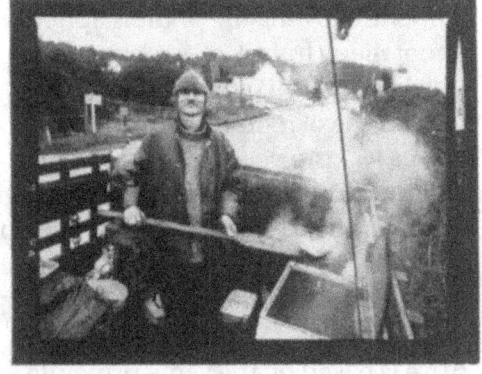

6x5

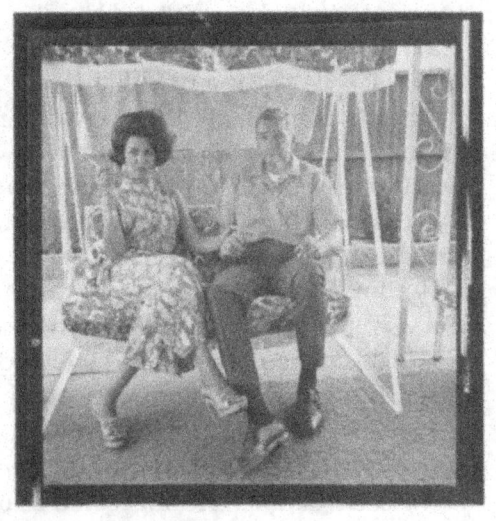

6x6

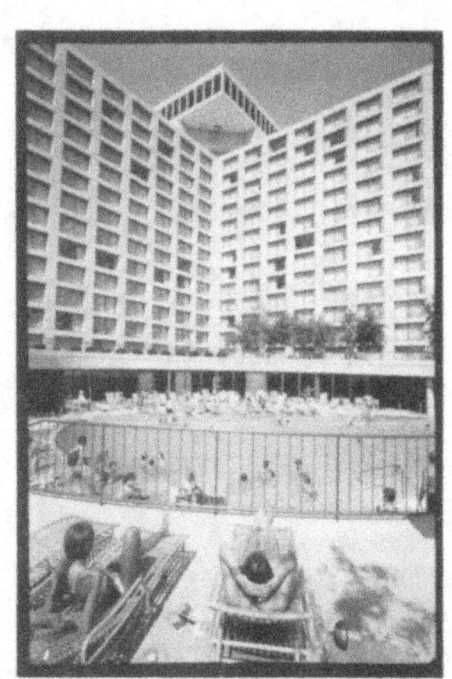

6x9

and strobe lights. I felt it was worth trying, so I purchased an array of strobe lights and a Pentax 6 x 7 camera. When on assignment for the newspaper, I continued to use a 35mm camera, but I started using the large camera for my documentary projects.

Many of the large format cameras use 120-220 film. I enjoy looking at prints made from these larger negatives because they are sharper and they provide a delicacy of detail which yields a certain richness of information about the subject. The reason for this is directly related to the correspondingly larger negative. The 6 x 7 camera uses a negative that need only be blown up four times to produce an 8 x 10 photographic print. To produce the same size print using 35mm film, the negative must be blown up eight times. The resulting sharp, tonally-rich prints reproduce well in magazines and books.

The use of another large format camera, the 4 x 5, brings with it a couple of drawbacks. It requires a tripod and is extremely slow to operate. Moreover, using a tripod can't help but strongly shape your photographic style because of the limitations imposed upon placement of the camera. This is a severe limitation because it is often necessary in journalistic photography to be in the middle of the action and be able to move in quickly on interesting subjects.

The popular "personality" magazines are a perfect example of 35mm photography at its most mediocre. All the images in such magazines look boringly alike. This is because the pictures have been homogenized by certain camera techniques and poor quality magazine reproduction. The situation is not helped by the fact that most of the photographers sent out on this sort of

assignment aren't able to spend much time with their subjects. They shoot and run (aided by motor driven cameras), probably never seeing the subject again. They know that with 35mm cameras it is easy and fast to get the "right" photo; i.e., one the photo editor will like.

In contrast to this sort of photography, note the photograph of the woman in her kitchen. It was taken with a Pentax 6 x 7. I used a bounce strobe light to get the effect I wanted and had to guess at the exposure (about f-8). Even so, this photograph is so sharp that you can read the Betty Crocker Cook Book. There are many instances in which the use of strobe lighting is essential if you want to produce an image that can be easily read. (This is discussed in more detail in the "Lighting" section of this book.) But there is no one method of lighting a subject, and there are situations in which the use of natural light alone adds a lot to the "mood" of the photo. It's a good idea to familiarize yourself with all types of photographic equipment and techniques, as they are all tools of the trade.

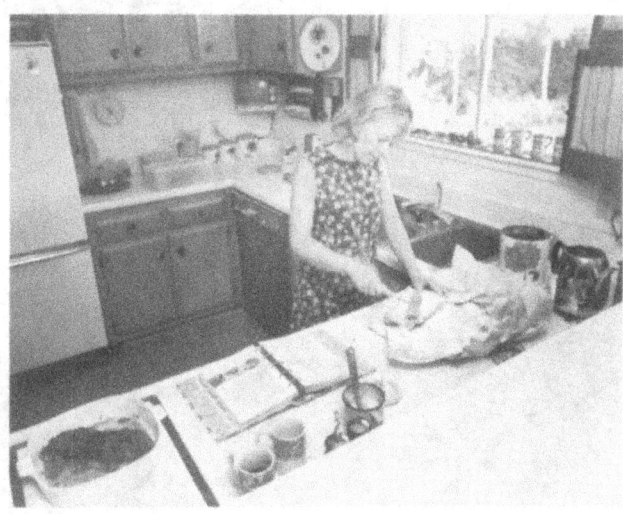

The psychological effect of working with a large camera is undeniable. (Not so much on yourself as on the people around you.) When someone sees me working with a camera that weights almost ten pounds, he assumes immediately that I'm a serious photographer. You are taken seriously when you work with a large camera, and that can prove to be a real asset. People often ask questions about what you're trying to do or even about the camera itself. And as it turns out, the people who come up to talk to me usually end up as my photographic subjects.

Another way to look like a professional photographer is to carry around five Nikons and wear a safari jacket.

It does look impressive; the Nikons also weigh more and take up more space than a Pentax 6x7 with two lenses.

Suburbia and my other books were done with large format cameras, wide angle lenses and strobe lights. This combination of photographic equipment allows me to control the tone of the final photographic print. In the documentary tradition, you must be able to "read" and comprehend the photograph. And so I require sharp photographs with rich middle greys; this kind of printing communicates information without over-dramatizing the subject. It's the sharpness of my photographs that marks my style—and *style* is what the photographic business is all about.

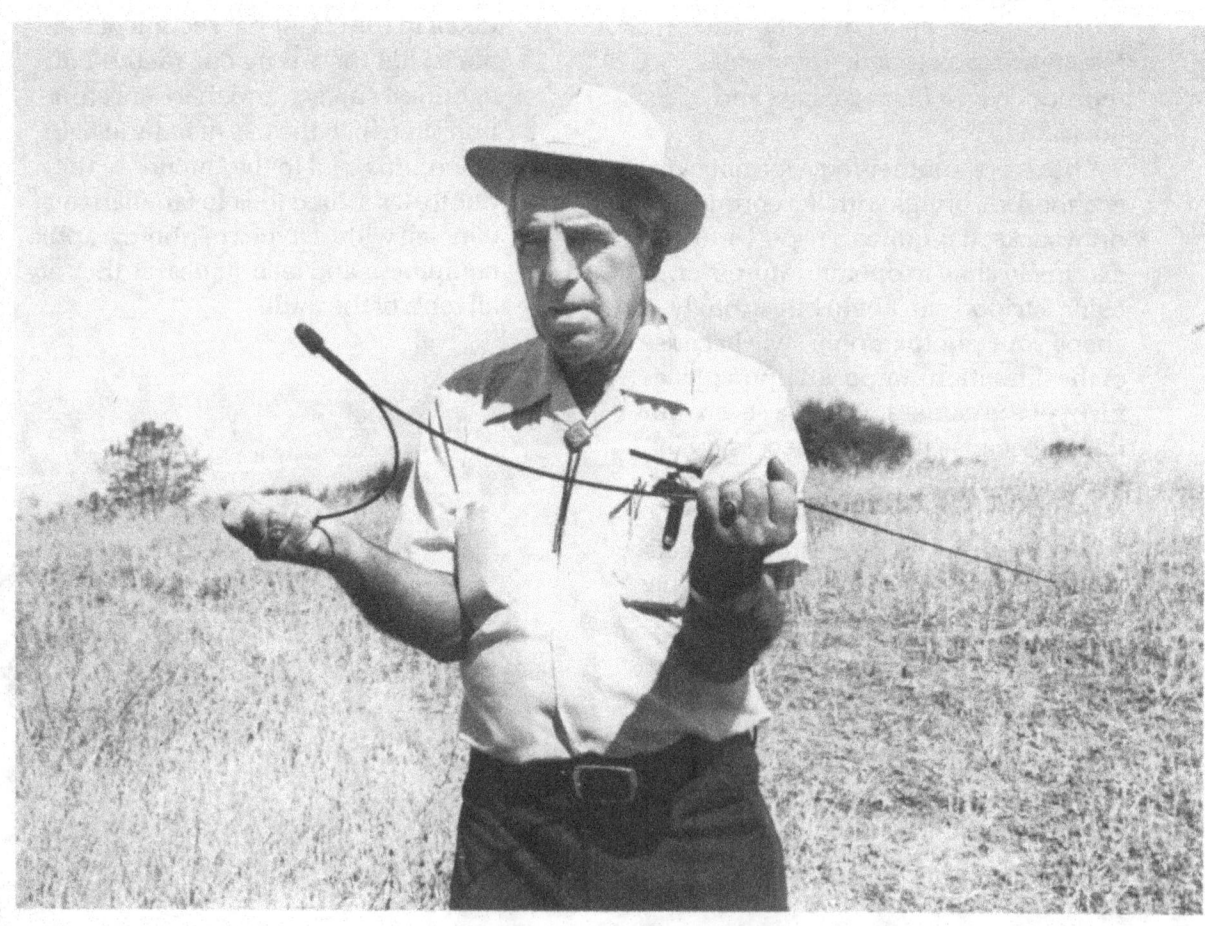

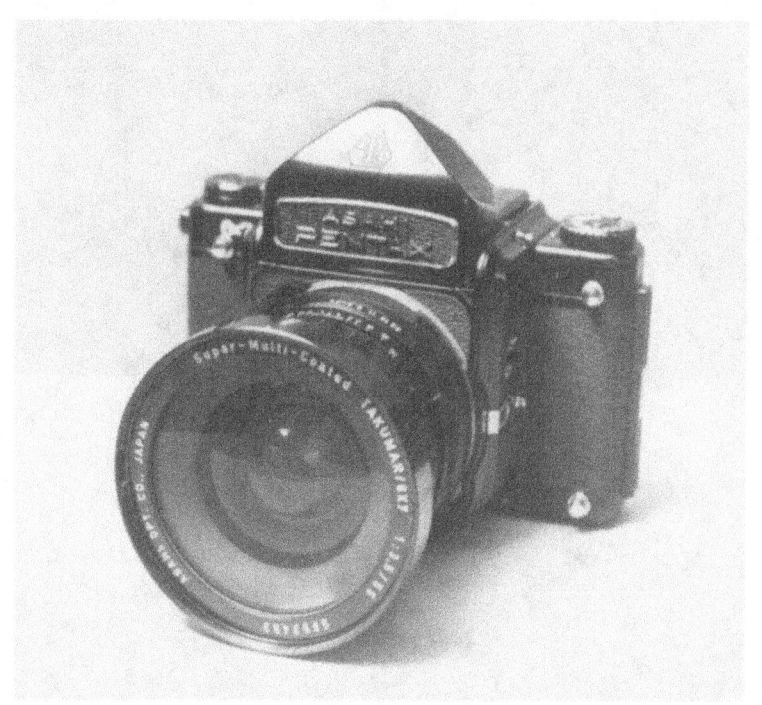

Pentax 6χ7

Bronica ETR

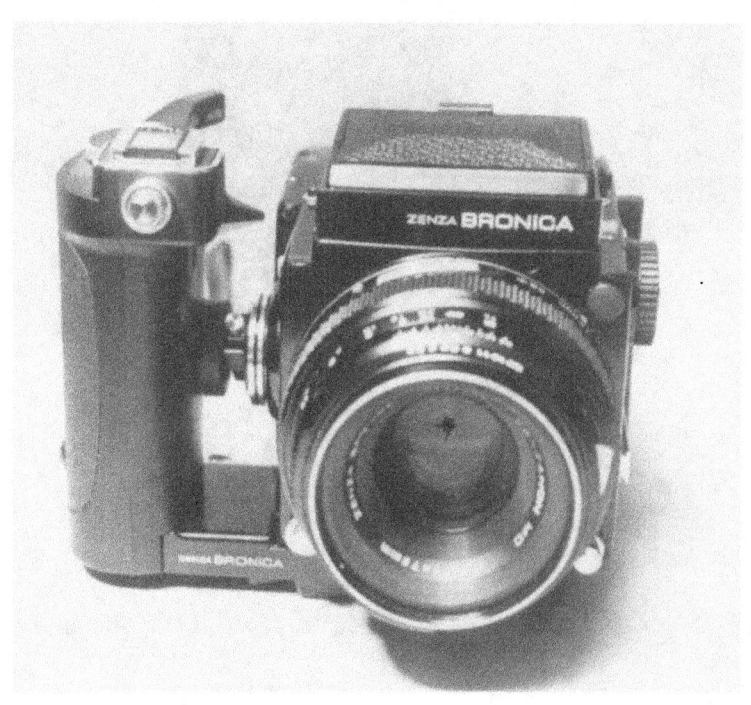

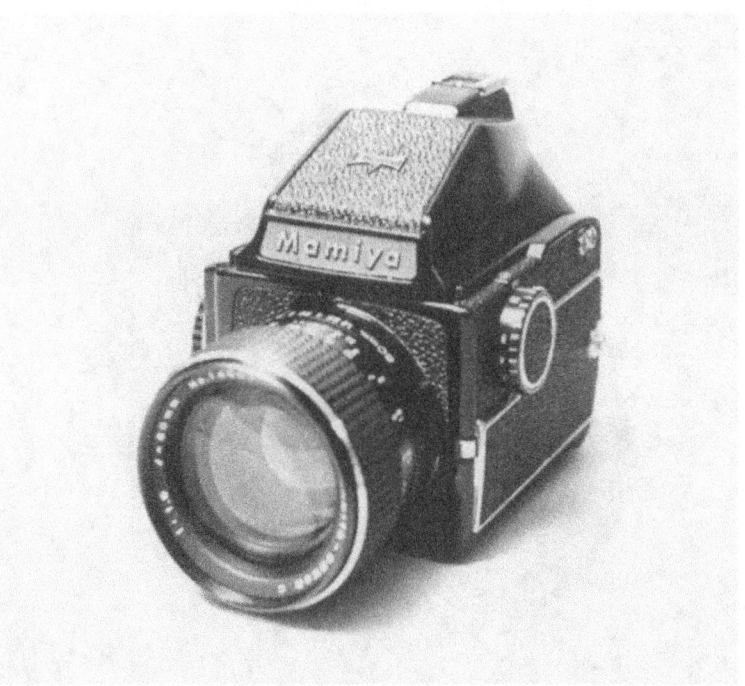

Mamiya

Mamiya RB67

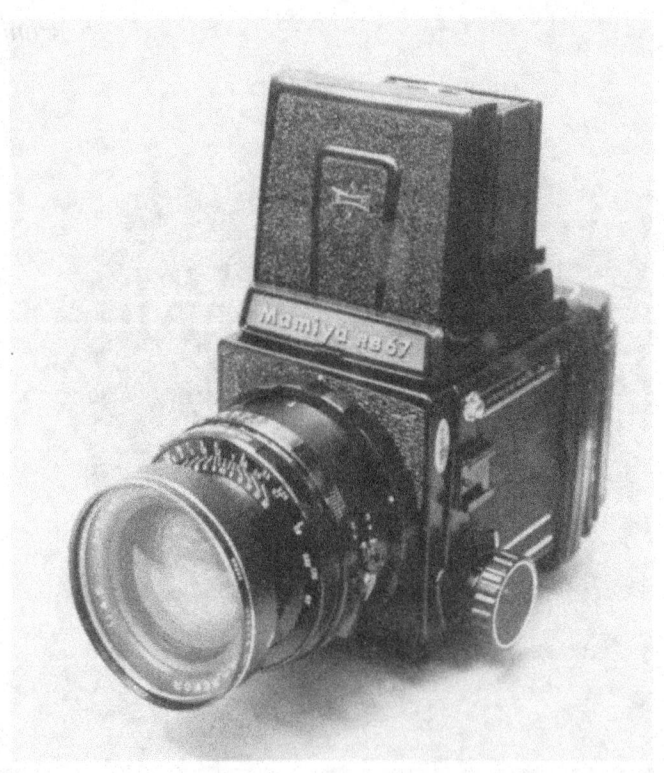

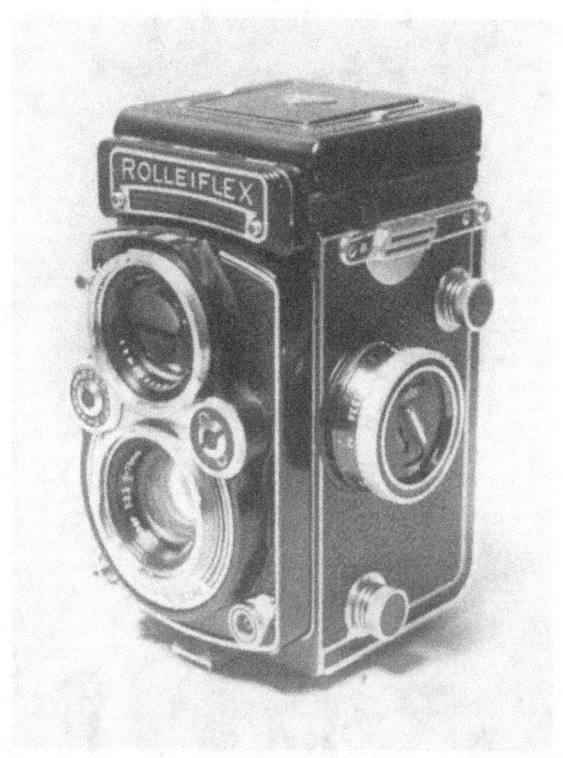

Rolleiflex

Technika PRP 55

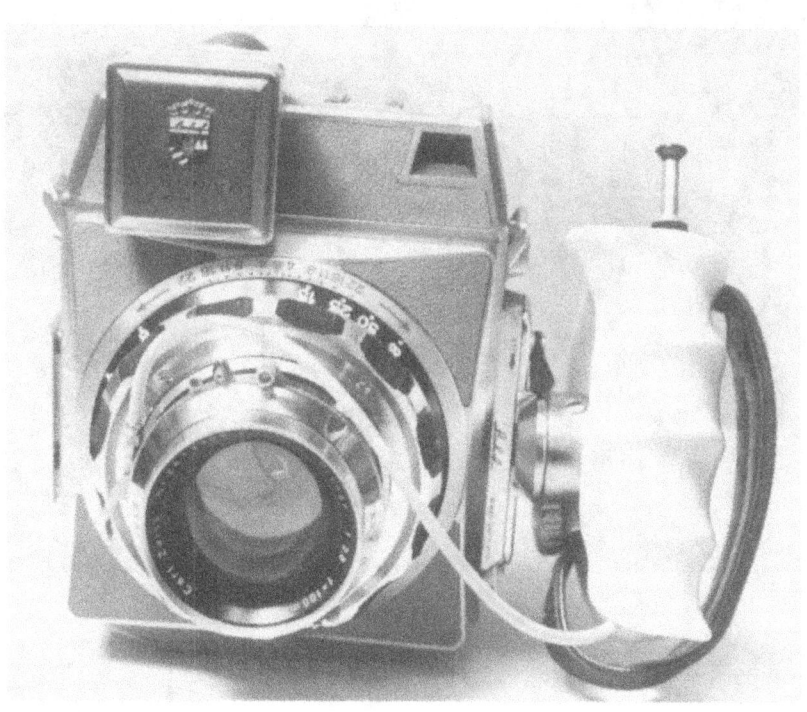

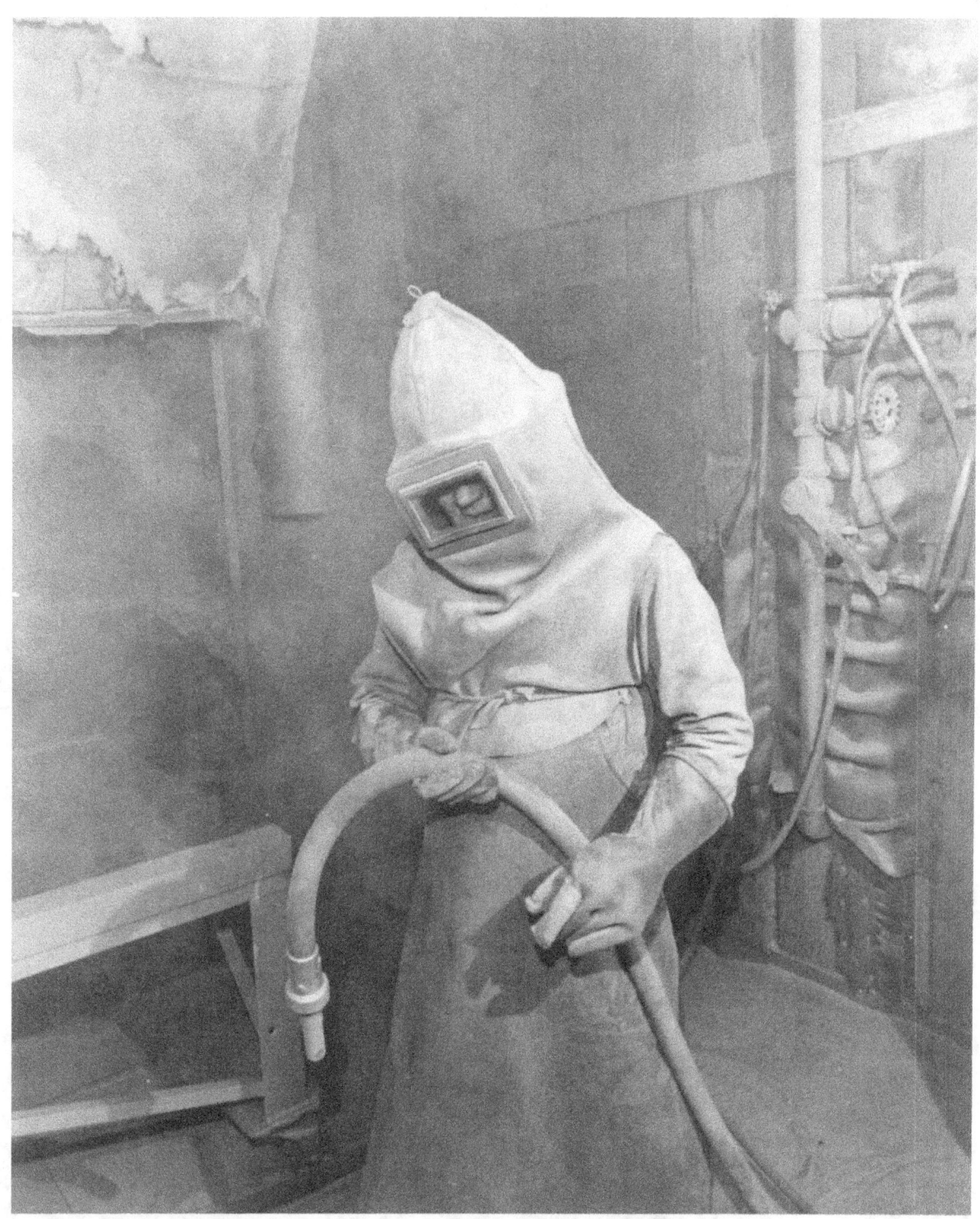

lighting

There are four basic lighting situations which a professional photographer should know how to handle. They are: direct light, back lighting, open shade and the use of strobe lighting in any or all of these situations.

Direct light falling onto a subject creates high contrasts (bright whites and dark shadows). Direct light is usually the worst sort of lighting for portraits, and except for a few special circumstances, it's best to avoid shooting in direct sunlight altogether. But sometimes you just get stuck and have to make the best of a bad lighting situation.

Knowing how to use the Zone system, developed by the great California photographer, Ansel Adams, can help a great deal when shooting in bright sunlight. If you are not familiar with the Zone system, simply bracket: take one picture at the apparently correct exposure, a second at one f-stop greater than the first, and a third at one f-stop less. Then select the negative which gives the greatest tonal range in the finished photograph.

Photographing in bright sunlight presents a difficult problem. These two photographs serve as an example. In the photograph on the left, the subjects' shoulders are reflecting the bright sunlight while their faces are hidden in deep shadow. There is a difference of about five stops between the bright and dark areas. If these photographs had been made with a 35mm camera, it's quite likely they would have been contrasty and lacked detail in the shadows. I made these photographs, though, using a large camera, because the larger negative gives more area in which to dodge and burn in the print. The larger negative can also produce prints which are sharper and less grainy than those

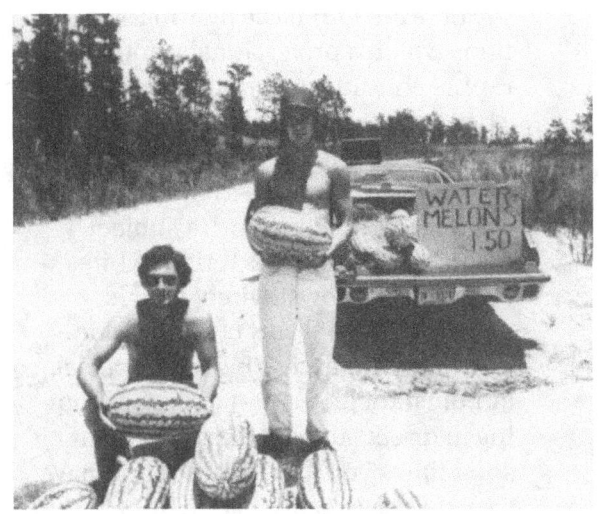 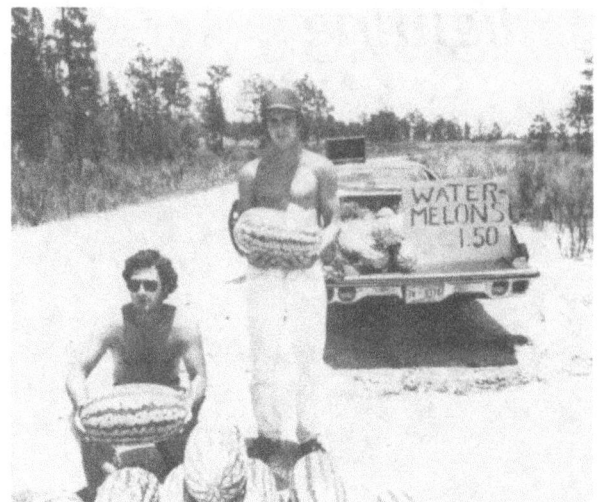

produced by a 35mm negative. In my opinion, 35mm film just can't hold up in quality (in bright sun situations) when compared to the 2 1/4 negative.

There are several ways to overcome the problems created by bright sun and deep shadows. The most immediately useful method is the Zone system. Because overexposure is not usually as difficult a problem as underexposure, the old advice still holds: expose for the shadows and develop for the highlights. When using Tri-X film, ASA 400, simply rate the film at ASA 200, thus overexposing by one stop. Then develop the film at 70% of the normal time. For example, if you use D76 developer at 68°, develop the film for 5 minutes instead of the standard 7 1/2 minutes. The development times are approximate and require experimentation. I think that Tri-X is the best film to use in bright sun because it has the widest latitude for overexposure and underdeveloping . . . try it!

Using a fill-in flash, deep shadows in bright sun can be practically eliminated. (The depth and placement of shadows can be varied for creative effect.) I recommend using a camera with a leaf shutter for this sort of thing—a Rollei, Hasselblad, or Bronica ETR. Used in conjunction with a fill-in flash, the shutter enables you to shoot at 1/500 at f-16.

If you don't have access to any of the cameras I mentioned above, then simply mount a fill-on flash on a 35mm camera and take the picture at 1/60 at f-11. The best film to use is Kodak Panatomic-X, ASA 32. This film had been taken off the market but is available once again.

Back lighting, light directed from behind the subject, often softens the subject and produces good modeling of features. Natural back lighting occurs in the morning and late afternoon. As with direct light, back lighting can present a high contrast situation, but in portraiture the use of back lighting can often make the subject more visually interesting. Once again, it's necessary to bracket several f-stops to get the right exposure.

Open shade is any lighting situation in which the sun doesn't directly illuminate the subject. It can be under a tree, in the shade of a building, or wherever the sun is obscured.

I think the best outdoor lighting occurs when the sun is hidden by high cirrus clouds, which gives a soft, indirect light. (I've waited as long as three weeks just to photograph on such a day.) There are no shadows to contend with, and often the light will be as bright as it would be in direct sunlight.

The open shade effect can also be obtained by waiting until just a few minutes before sunset. At that time, there are about fifteen minutes of soft, bright light in which to shoot. I recommend using an average exposure of 1/250 at f-16 with Tri-X film when photographing in open shade.

Strobe lighting is necessary whenever the available light is insufficient to expose the film, or when a photog-

rapher wants to bring out certain textures and add depth to his photographs. It is the ability to use strobe light that separates the professional photographer from the "art crowd" photographer. A professional photographer should know how to use the four basic types of strobe lighting— direct strobe, bounce strobe, bare tube strobe (reflectorless flash), and a Norman or Balcar 50 to 100 watt-second electronic power unit with an umbrella. Knowing how to properly light your subject is a matter, once again, of learning by doing. There is no other way!

I suggest first asking a studio photographer to show you how to operate his strobe lighting equipment. Most studio photographers will be happy to share this information with you. You may even learn how to use a five-head 10,000 watt-second strobe unit! Then you will

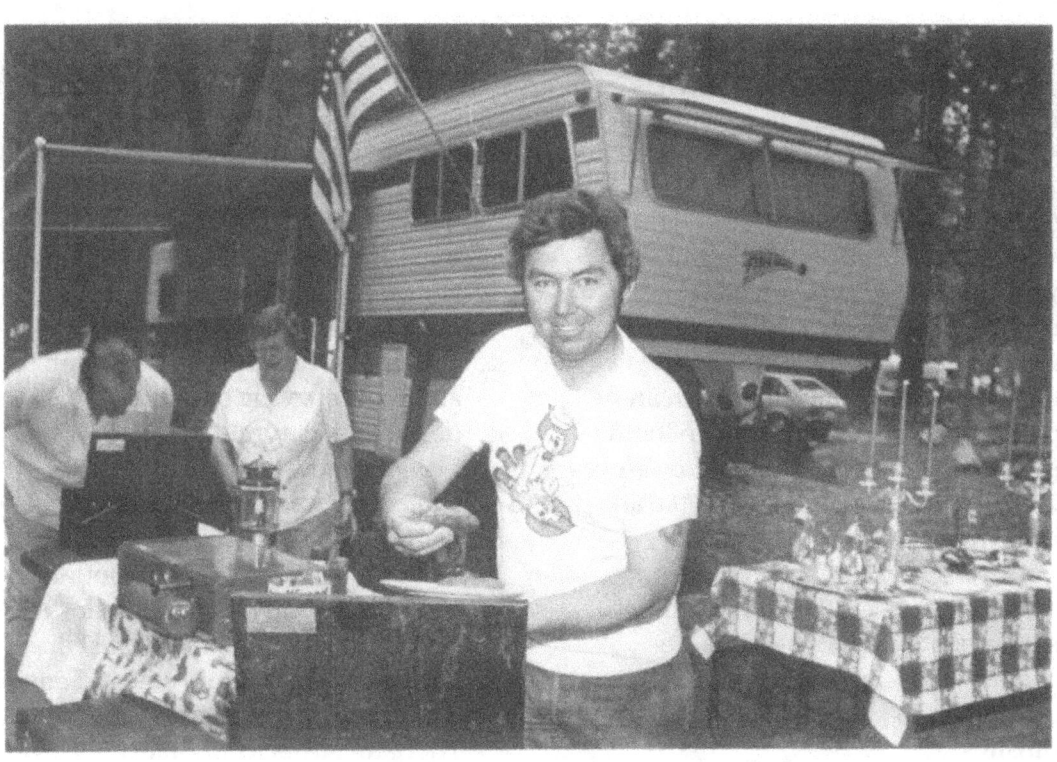

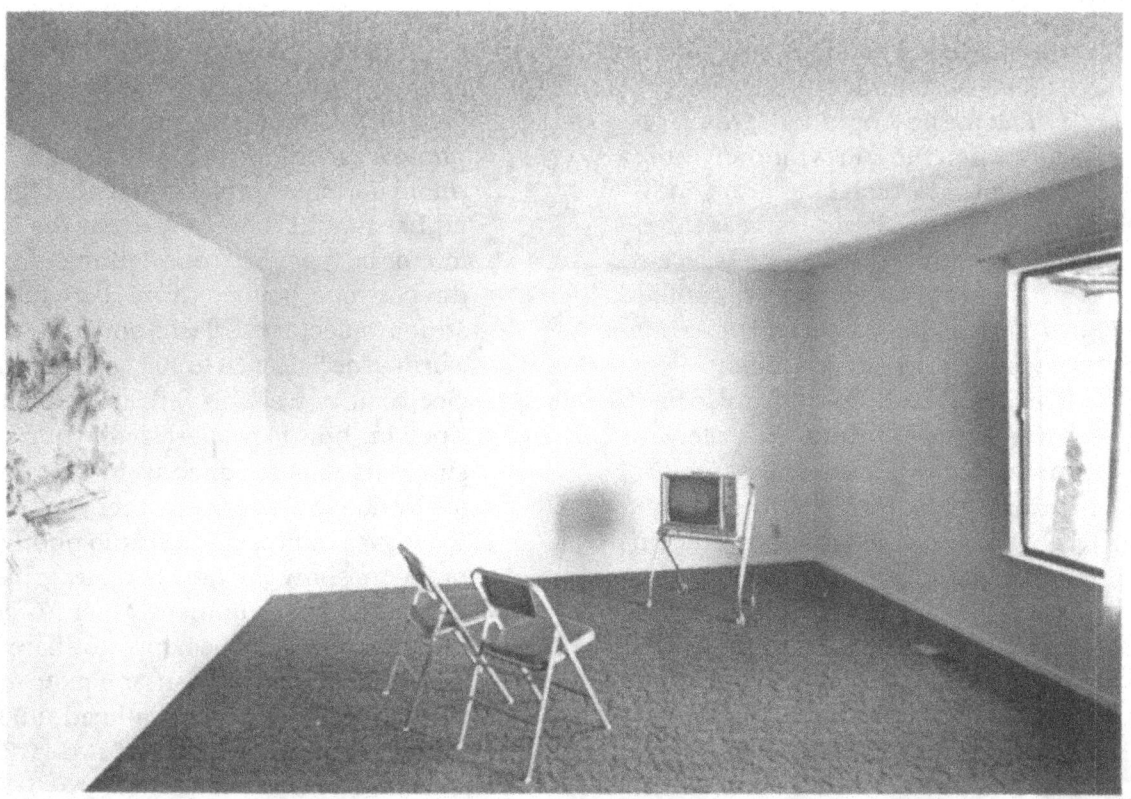

probably need to acquire your own equipment. Any camera store worth its salt will have strobe equipment to sell or rent.

Once acquainted with the basics of strobe lighting, the only way to find out what a camera and strobe unit will actually do is to shoot a test roll of film. It's that simple. I've encountered many so-called photographers who own an expensive camera but are afraid of both the camera and the flash unit. They are probably afraid of people too. . . . (I think this is why so many photographers shoot landscapes, buildings, children, flowers, and sunsets. I believe it's much easier to photograph Yosemite's tremendous landscapes than it is to photograph the people in the campsites.)

Direct flash is the simplest and quickest method. Most strobe lighting is done in this way because today's electronic strobes with thyristor circuits have taken the guesswork out of photography. (You just have to follow the instructions.) However, there is a big drawback in using direct flash exclusively—the resulting print is often flat and uninteresting because of a lack of depth and texture.

Bounce strobe is a way of lighting a subject indirectly. A photograph taken using bounce strobe appears to have been taken in natural light. Bounce strobe is the most difficult to do, but the results are often the most satisfying because the light looks soft and natural and gives full-tone negatives. Many new Thyristor strobes now allow one to aim the strobe at the ceiling to get the bounced light effect. However, the Thyristor circuit works well *only* in small rooms. (For professional results, purchase a 100 or 200 watt-second strobe and a flash meter.) Be extremely careful and bracket each time you shoot. Otherwise, you may come up with nothing on the film at all. Practice using strobes in various circumstances, from total darkness to half-lit rooms.

These photographs illustrate the difference between the use of natural light and strobe light. The photograph on the left was taken with natural light. The print is 40% black; half the man's face is in deep shadow. As you can see, the print is dark and contrasty. And the

high contrast presents the couple in an unattractive way. Both their faces are lit dramatically, and the woman's hand looks more like a claw than a hand.

The strobe lit photograph on the right reverses the situation. Both faces are well lit, and one can see textures in their hair and clothing. The shadows now serve to define rather than distort, and a more even three dimensional quality is created in the image. If *Suburbia* had been photographed with natural light exclusively, the deep shadow effect would have dominated the book, and it would have been difficult to read many of the photographs. (As it was, too many people thought *Suburbia* was a put-down of suburban life styles.)

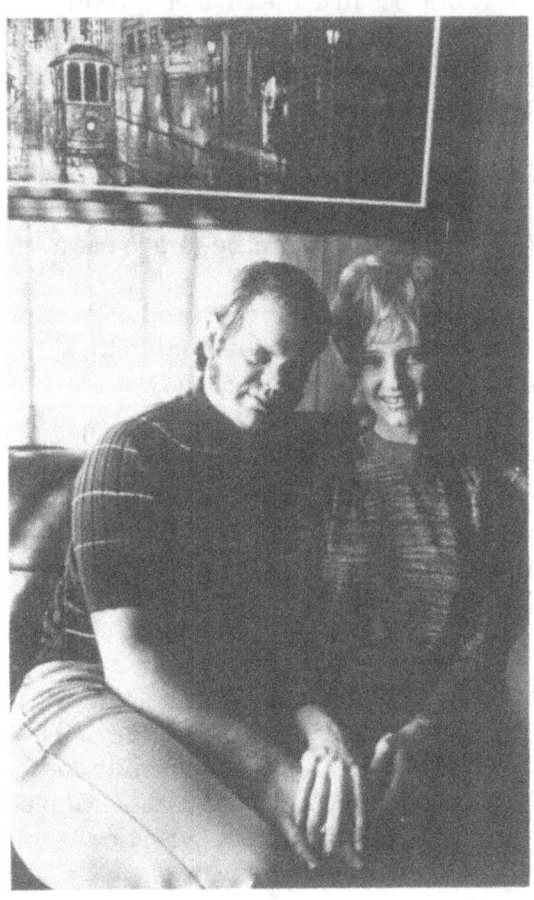
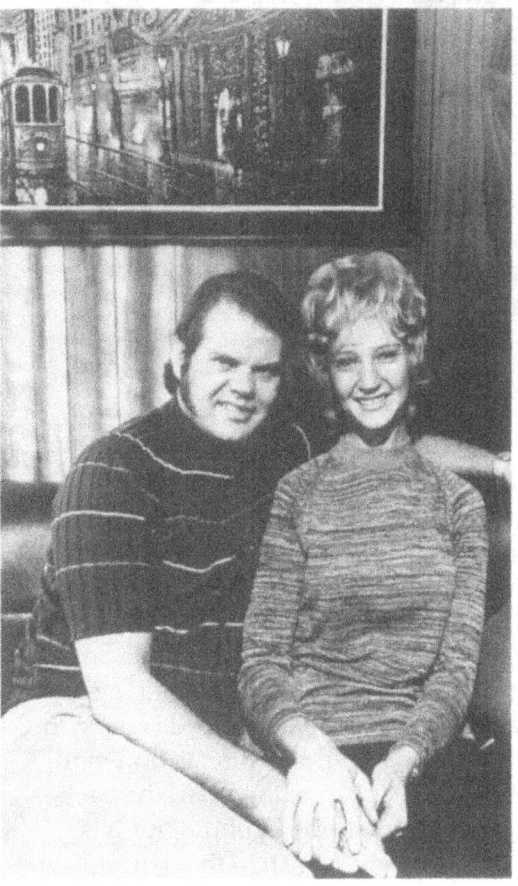

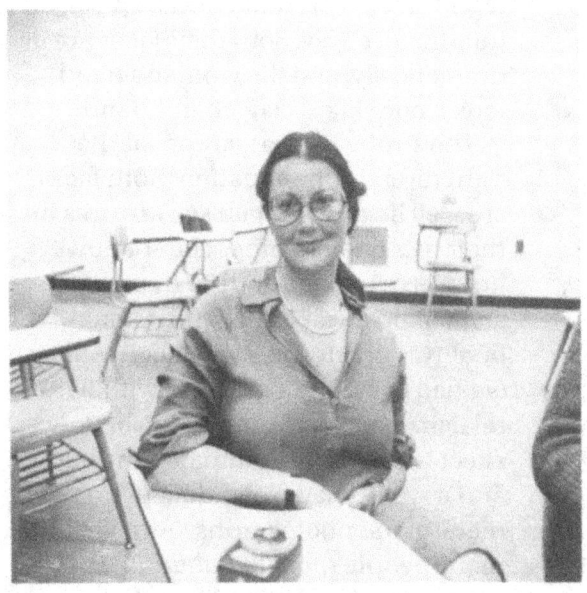 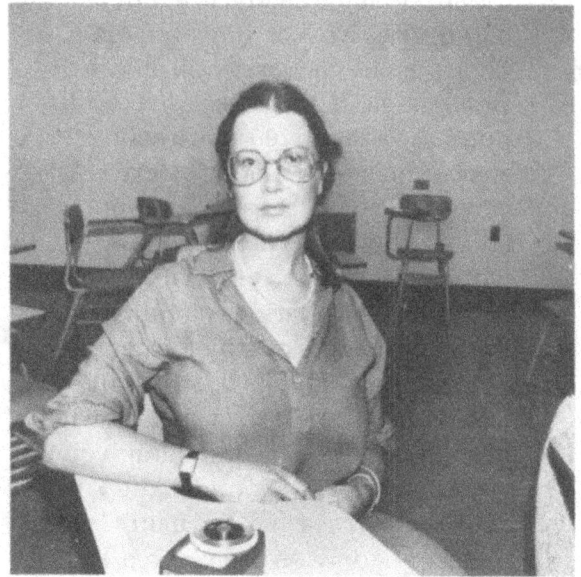

The bare tube strobe is a useful tool when shooting where fluorescent lights are the predominant light source. (Most schools, offices, factories, supermarkets, and some homes.)

The reflectorless flash of bare tube strobes allows light to radiate in all directions. The resulting light reflects off walls and the ceiling, adding depth and softening the shadows in the photograph.

The photograph taken in natural light was shot at 1/125 at f-4 with Tri-X film. The subject is dark and indistinct. One's eyes are drawn to the bright area behind the subject rather than to the subject. The other photograph was taken at 1/250 at f-16 using a bare tube strobe. The light from the bare tube strobe dramatically alters the photograph. The subject is well lit and clearly defined, and the background is dark. In this photograph, attention is drawn to the woman's face rather than the background. The strobe lit photograph is also much sharper than the naturally lit

one because the smaller aperture (f-16) gives a greater depth of field.

The best way to arrange the lighting in this situation is to have one reflectorless flash mounted on the camera and a second bare tube strobe (a slave unit) set up on a light stand. To get the proper exposure, be sure to use a strobe meter.

The most thorough and professional way to light any interior is with a *Norman* or *Balcar* 50 to 1200 watt-second electronic power unit. These powerful units enable one to bounce lights off umbrellas or off the ceiling, usually producing beautiful full-tone negatives. As with the bare tube strobe, using a strobe meter is absolutely essential.

Strobe lighting is an integral part of documentary photography. As I've already mentioned several times, there are many times when you must use a flash meter to get good results. Its use can spare you a great deal of trouble and bad exposures. If you are planning to do a documentary project, I suggest that you buy a 200 watt-second strobe light and a flash meter.

While working on *Suburbia*, I used a bounce light strobe. But I had to bracket each exposure because I didn't use a strobe meter. Consequently, many of the negatives were exposed incorrectly. It wasn't a very smart way to handle it when an $80 flash meter could have solved all of my lighting problems. I'm appalled at the number of people who call themselves photographers but are unable to use strobe lights. These people have locked themselves into one way of working. Many of them are afraid to move into a more professional level of photography.

If you find that all this strobe lighting and metering is too complicated for you, then I suggest that you purchase a 750 watt quartz light and a light stand. (This will cost about $120.) A quartz light unit can light most interiors with a soft, natural-looking light, and produce full-tone negatives with rich middle greys. Quartz lights are easy to use. Simply bounce the light off the ceiling and use a hand held reflective light meter to determine proper exposures. Be careful on one point, however. Quartz lights are very hot, and the intense heat from the lamp can easily burn the paint on the ceiling. (I should know!) About one third of the photographs in *Suburbia* were taken with quartz lights. The use of the large camera, wide-angle lenses, and quartz lights helped to create my photographic style.

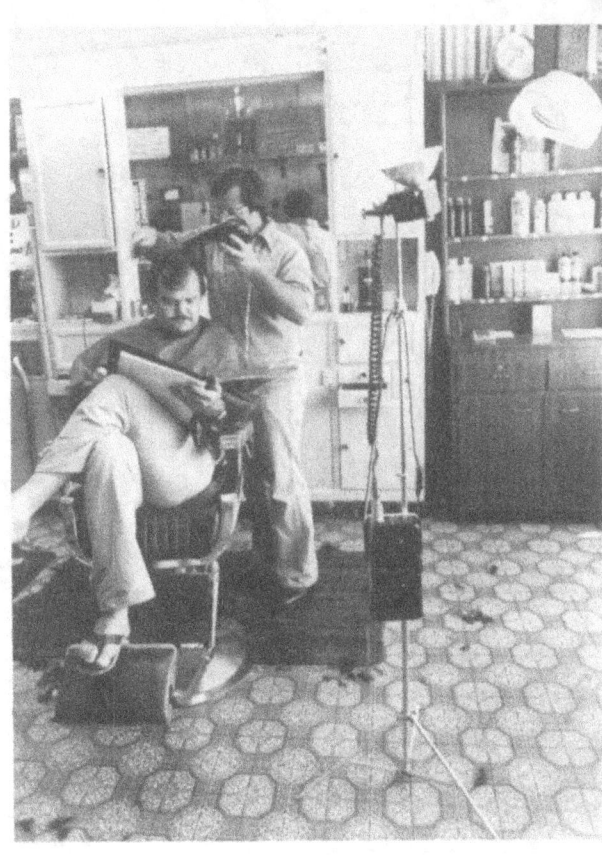

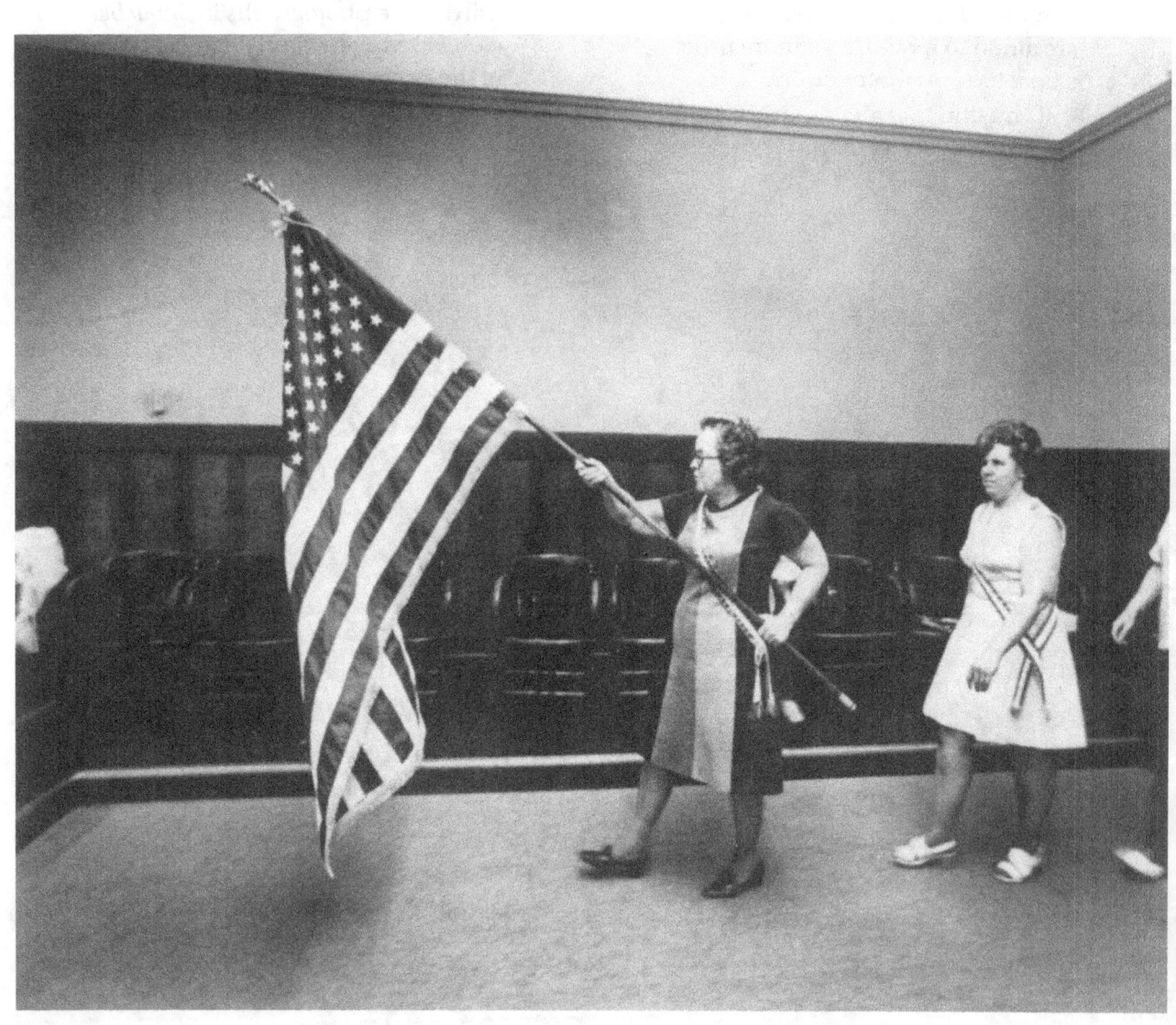

the documentary photograph

If a documentary photograph is to have any life in it, it's very important that it exhibit certain characteristics. The photograph should, first of all, be about people. Nothing is more fascinating than the human face and the human condition. A photographer must then choose between taking a posed photograph and a candid one. (80% of the pictures in *Suburbia* are posed, the rest are still-life shots or candid photographs.)

The candid photograph usually gives us the most insight into the character of a subject. In a candid photograph, a photographer is able to capture more accurately particular attitudes and qualities of a subject. Unfortunately, the candid photograph is the most difficult to make. In the first place, the photographer has to be practically invisible. Next, he needs an acute sense of timing in order to take the photograph at the "decisive moment." The ability to be in the right place at the right time is a rare gift. That's why most of us fall back on the posed picture, probably ending up with a static or merely random image. This is often characteristic of snapshots and some 4x5 camera work.

A documentary photograph of this particular type should contain information about how people live, work, and play. For example, the close-up of the newlyweds fails to give that information. Their pose is obviously forced and unnatural—they are simply mugging. However, the second photograph (taken with a wide-angle lens) encompasses the whole room and is full of life. Though posed, it contains a great deal of information about the young couple; and it's the quality and coherence of the information in any photograph that gives life to the image.

Take a few moments to notice all the

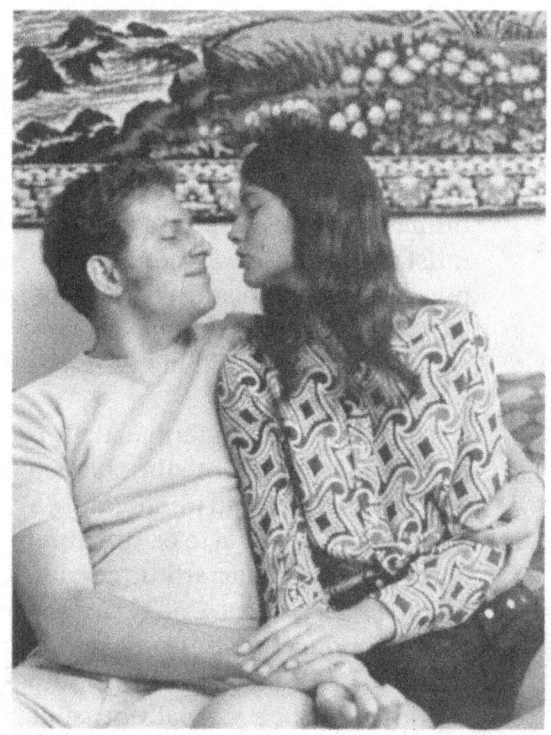
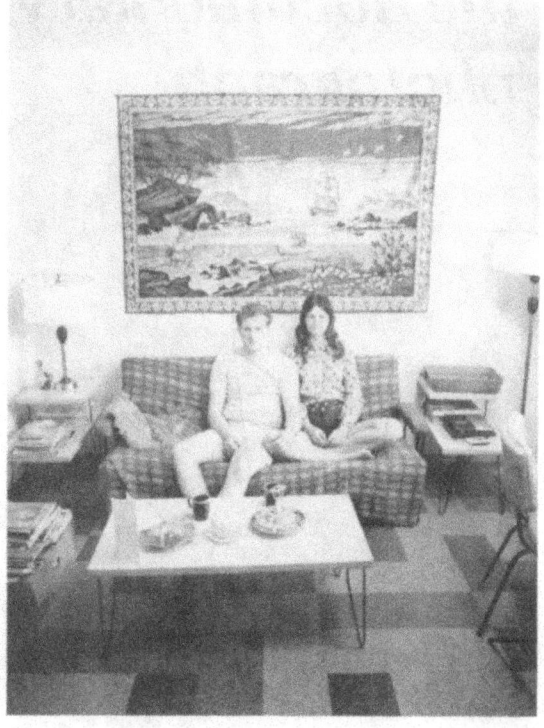

information conveyed by this photograph. Both of them are dressed informally, but his position relative to her,
with his shoulder firmly in front, seems
to indicate his dominant position.
(They both wear shorts, but he wears
the pants in the family.) The room is fur-
nished with blond furniture, and popu-
lated with knick-knacks, coffee cups,
Playboy magazines, a tape recorder, a
plastic container for their pet turtle and
a bargain basement tapestry. (My
450 watt quartz light, placed next to the
window to approximate natural light, is
just out of sight on the far right.) The
things the couple has chosen to place
in their living room say to others, "This
is who we are." A final note about this
photograph: This couple answered my
advertisement in the newspaper in
which I asked to "photograph people

living in suburbia." They phoned *me*,
which made the situation very open
and cooperative. It only took an hour to
get the picture I wanted.

The technical know-how necessary
to find the right people and location,
and to choose the right camera and
lighting system for the job, comes only
with experience. Only a moment's difference, and a lot of attention to detail,
separates the lowly snapshot from the
documentary photograph. Even something as ordinary as a birthday party
can serve to demonstrate the difference
between the two. A documentary
photograph must go beyond being simply a record of an event, and make a
clear statement about the subject and
his situation. This photograph of the
birthday party remains firmly in the category of a snapshot for two reasons.

The first is a matter of timing. The photograph was taken just a moment too late, so the girl in the background is perfectly in focus but the intended subject of the picture is not. And secondly, strobe lights—probably a bounce strobe—should have been used to freeze the action and modify the available lighting.

If an advertising photographer were shooting the same scene, he would simply arrange it to his liking and shoot three or four rolls of film until he got what he wanted. The poor girl would probably have to blow out the candles a dozen times. But the documentary photographer doesn't have that option; he must anticipate circumstances before they unfold, and be ready to capture events as they happen.

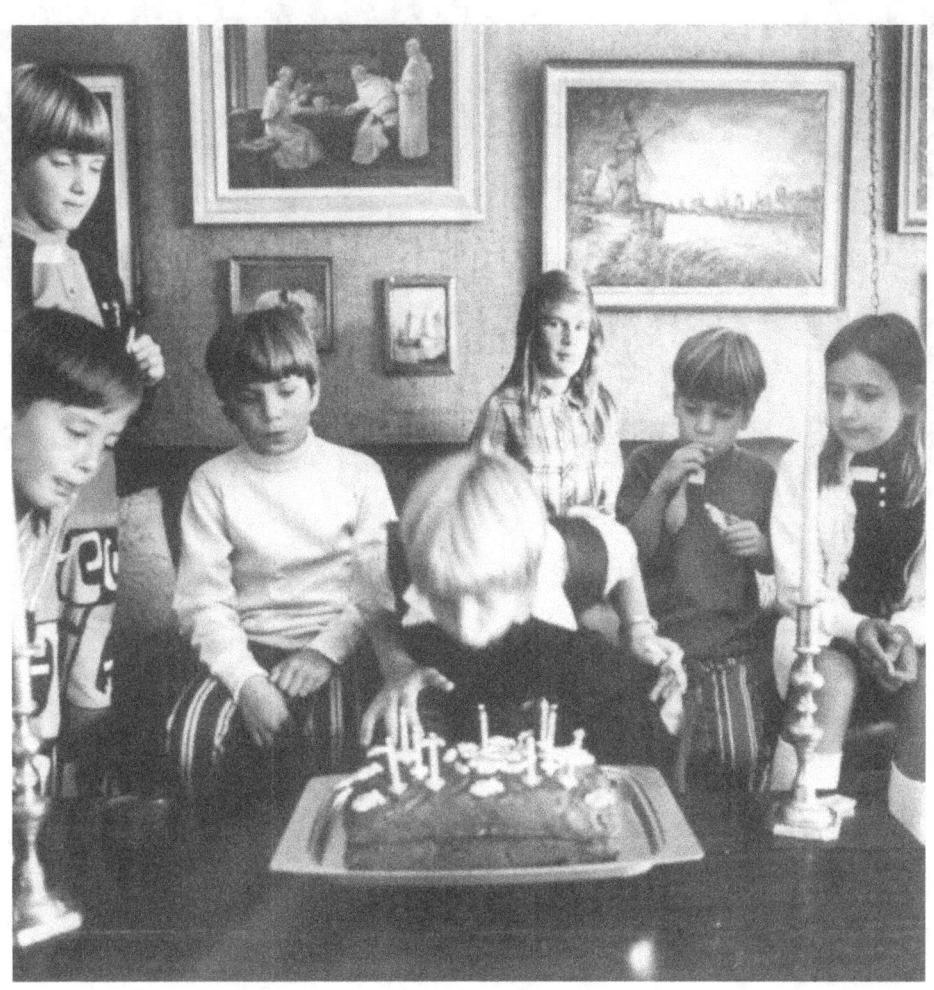

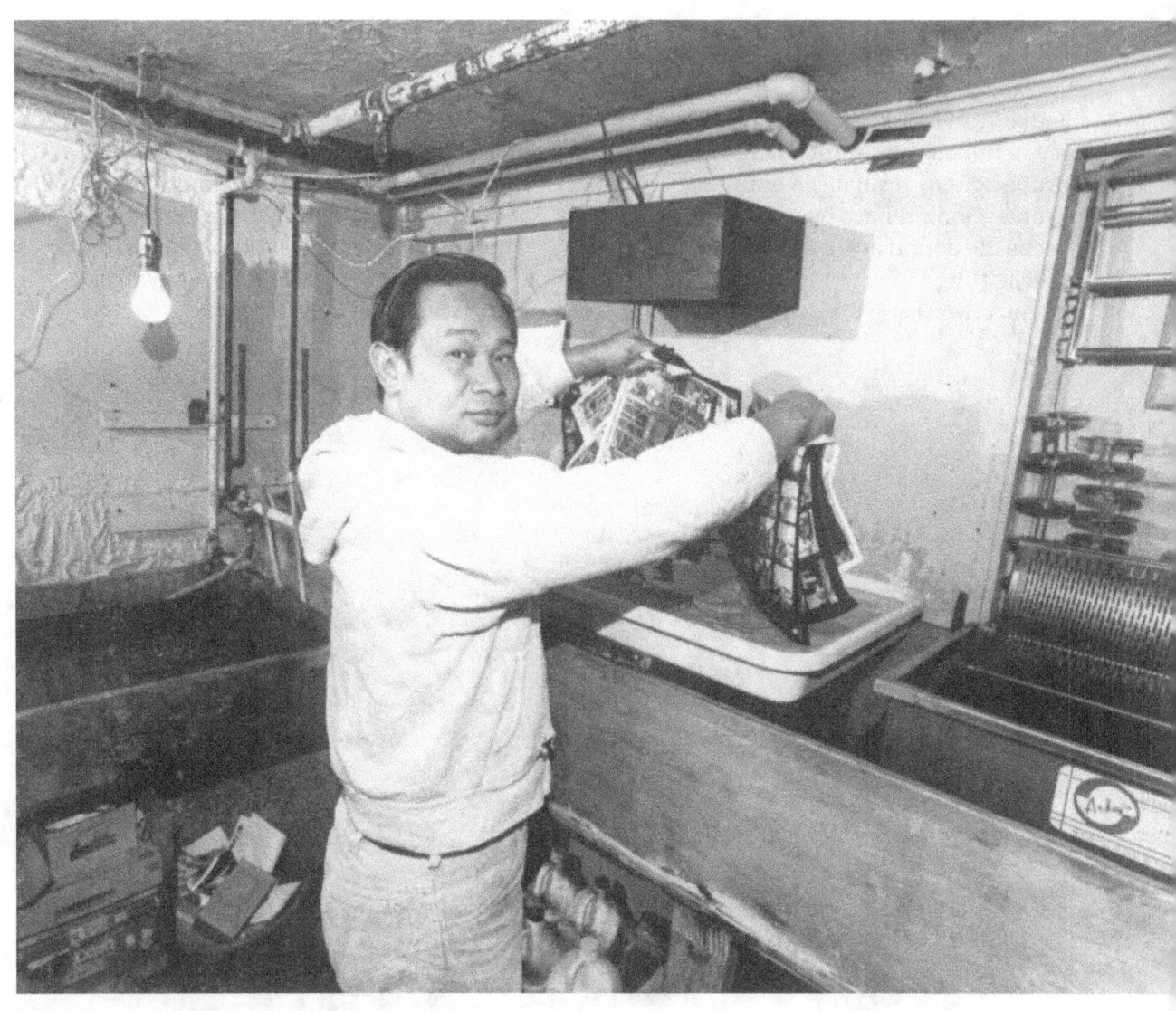

stock agencies

We live in an age of images. They proliferate. They look at us from every vantage point. There is hardly a place on the planet—or even the moon, for that matter—that hasn't been photographed by someone. One of the factors that led to the development of stock agencies was the growing need for storage and access to all these images (by periodicals of all sorts, publishers, scholars, etc.).

Stock agencies can be broken down into two types: there are some agencies that function principally as repositories for photographs—true visual libraries; there are others that, while serving as an image bank, are more actively engaged in representing their photographers. And there are many agencies with numerous variations of these functions.

How does an unknown photographer go about submitting material to stock agencies? The first thing to keep in mind is that you should never send material to an agency unsolicited. The proper procedure is to send a well-written letter to an agency of your choice. (For a complete listing of picture sources and stock agencies, consult *Picture Sources*, published by Special Library Association, and two R.R. Bowker publications, *Literary Marketplace* and *Photography Marketplace.* All these invaluable source books can be found in any library.) In the letter, explain what your subject matter generally consists of, and where you took most of your photographs. Also inform them as to what kind of equipment and what sort of film stock you work with.

You will then receive a reply based on that information. If you are invited to submit material, the agency will require two things of you. They will request that you send at least 200 samples of your work, which will be judged and systematically edited. If you work in color, send positive color transparencies; if in black and white, either contact sheets or prints will do. In addition, the agency will stipulate that you accept their standard contract. (There are far too many photographers submitting portfolios for them to have to quibble over who gets what percentage.)

It is only after this thorough screening process that a photographer's work may be accepted. There are rare instances when a particularly talented new photographer comes to the attention of a stock agency, and his or her work is solicited by that agency.

Photographs are sold to customers for one-time rights only, so it is possible for a given picture to be sold many times. When selling a relative newcomer's work, the fee is usually split 50/50. Even so, once a photographer's work has been accepted at a picture agency, he still can't accurately judge how well he is doing for at least three to five years! Don't be disappointed, then, if after a year nothing seems to be happening. It takes time for the process to come to fruition.

The national professional organization of stock agencies is called the *Picture Agency Council of America*. This organization sets the standards for the industry. Before you submit a letter to an agency, it's a good idea to make sure it belongs to the Picture Agency Council.

Picture Agency Council of America
P.O. Box 2063
Grand Central Station
New York, N.Y. 10017
President: Ms. Jane S. Kinne

PARTIAL LIST OF STOCK AGENCIES

Peter Arnold, Inc.
1500 Broadway, New York, NY 10036
Tel: (212) 840-6928
Contact: Peter Arnold
Specialties: abstract photomicrography, light and type patterns, nature, travel, science, sports.

Blackstar
450 Park Avenue South, New York, NY 10016
Tel: (212) 679-3288
Contact: Howard Chapnick
Specialties: diverse subjects, from American cities to war photos

Bruce Coleman, Inc.
150 East 36th St., New York, NY 10016
Tel: (212) 683-5227
Contact: Norman Tomalin
Specialties: geography, natural history, science

Design Photographers International
521 Madison Ave., New York, NY 10022
Tel: (212) 752-3930
Contact: Alfred Forsyth
Specialties: all subjects

Globe Photos
404 Park Avenue South, New York, NY 10016
Tel: (212) 689-1340
Contact: Gary Phillips
Specialties: advertising, moviestills, photojournalism

Image Bank
88 Vanderbilt Ave., New York, NY 10017
Tel: (212) 371-3636
Contact: Marty Abrams
Specialties: advertising, travel, special effects, sports

Magnum Photos, Inc.
15 West 46th St., New York, NY 10036
Tel: (212) 541-7570
Contact: Joan Lifton
Specialties: nature, science, social and political history, photojournalism, technology

Photo Researchers, Inc.
60 East 56th St., New York, NY 10022
Tel: (212) 758-3420
Contact: Jane S. Kinne
Specialties: comparative culture, psychology, social and natural history, geography

Shostal Associates
60 East 42nd St., New York, NY 10017
Tel: (212) 687-0696
Contact: David Forbert
Specialties: all subjects—U.S. & foreign

Sygma
322 West 46th St., New York, NY 10023
Tel: (212) 595-0077
Contact: E. Laffont
Specialties: aviation, photojournalism, special events, travel, war photos

Woodfin Camp & Associates, Inc.
30 Rockefeller Plaza, New York, NY 10020
Tel: (212) 489-7675
Contact: Woodfin Camp or Midge Keater
Specialties: aerials, food, fashion, industry, world geography

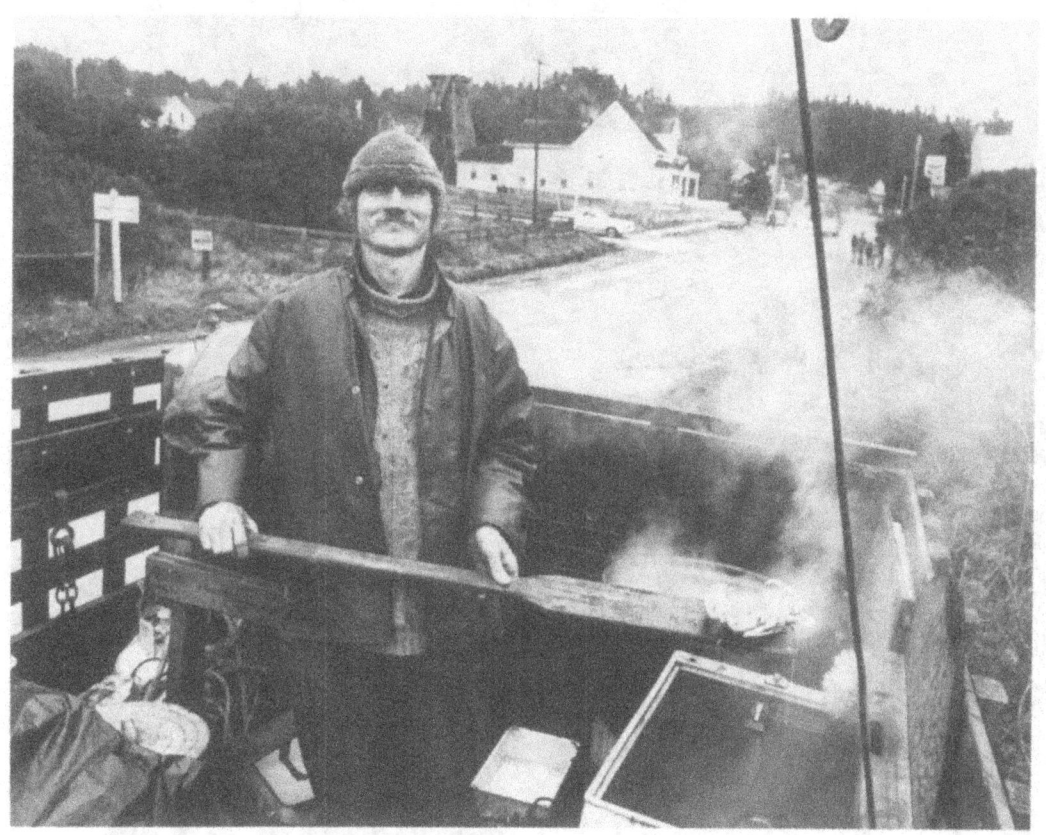

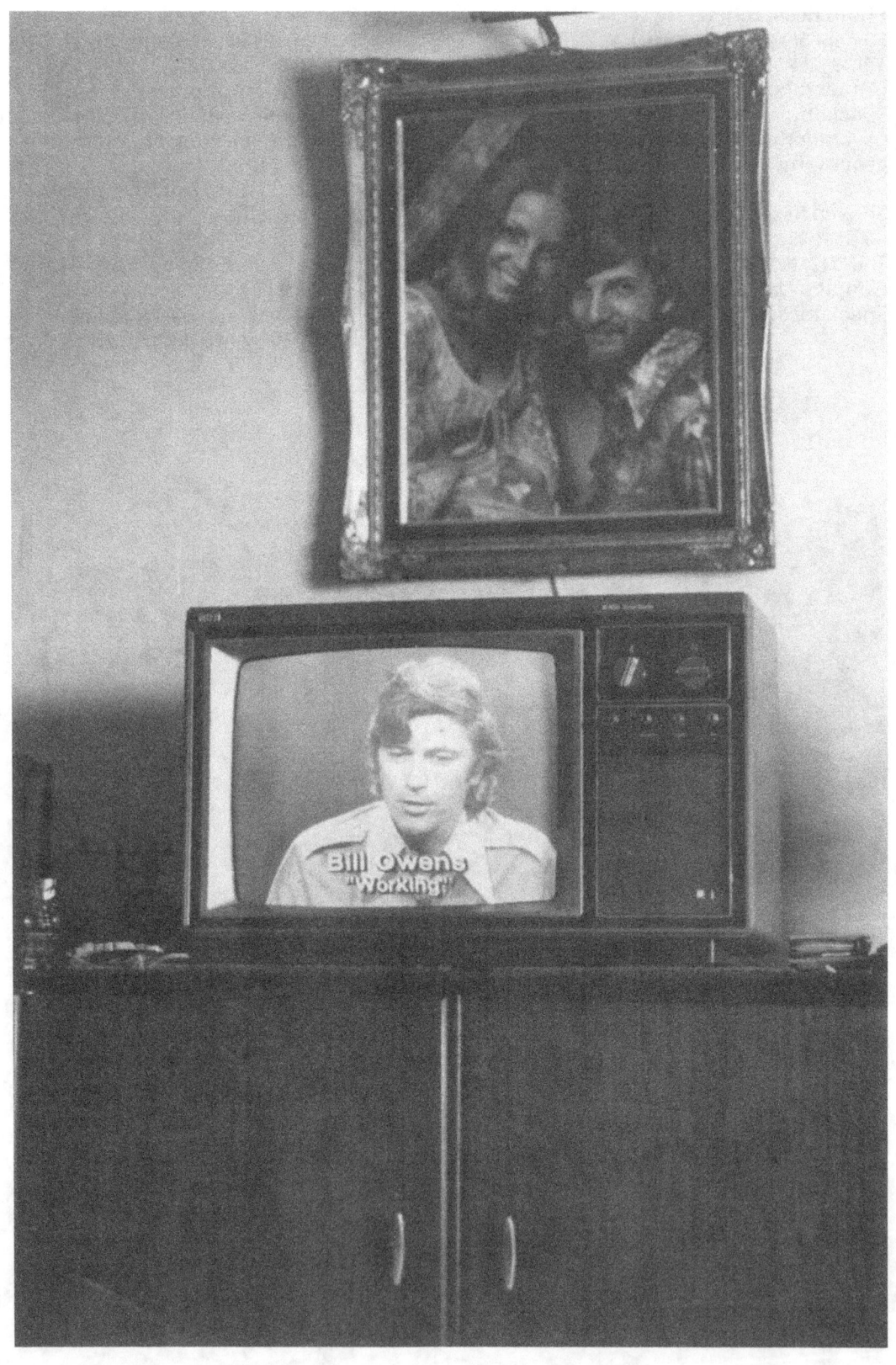

forms and applications

On the following pages are reproductions of the John Simon Guggenheim Foundation and the National Endowment for the Arts grant application forms, as well as my statement of work plans for *Suburbia, Our Kind of People,* and *Working (I Do It For The Money).* I have also included the statement of work plans for my present project on leisure as major part of the American way of life. The statement of work plans for *Working* was used to obtain a Guggenheim grant *and* a book advance. I received $12,000 from the Guggenheim Foundation and $5,000 from Simon & Schuster. The money supported me for the year it took to complete the project. The book required five months actual shooting time and seven months for planning and editing.

Because a publisher requires a beautiful set of prints and a well written proposal, as does any grant foundation, I use the same statements when submitting a book proposal and applying for a grant. Remember that grants are given to finance "photographic projects," not books. It's up to you to turn the project into a book by selling your work and your ideas to a publisher.

Photographers' Fellowships

To enable photographers to set aside time and purchase materials and generally to advance their careers as they see fit.

Eligibility

Photographers of exceptional talent of any age or aesthetic persuasion. Artists employing photography as the primary consideration in their work may also apply. (Students are not eligible.)

Grant Amount

$10,000.

The panel will recommend a limited number of $3,000 fellowships for emerging artists.

Deadline and Announcement Date

Applications must be postmarked no later than April 3, 1978. Applicants should not anticipate notification of awards or rejections before October 1978.

Period of activity should not be scheduled to begin before November 1978 and should be carried out during the succeeding twelve months.

Application Procedure

Please read carefully the following information and then review the instructions given on page 21 in order to complete the forms entitled *Individual Grant Application NEA-2 (Rev.).* In addition, complete the white cards and return them with your application.

Fellowship applications must be mailed to:

Grants Office
Visual Arts Fellowships
Mail Stop 701
National Endowment for the Arts
2401 E street, N.W.
Washington, D.C. 20506

Up to ten photographs and/or slides should be submitted with your application and will be returned. Recent work should be emphasized. While every effort will be made to insure safe handling of portfolios, the Endowment will not be responsible for any loss or damage. We urge you to exercise extreme care in packaging and labeling all materials sent through the mail. Your name, address, and the date of the work must appear on the back of each photograph submitted. **Because of difficulties in handling, portfolio boxes must not exceed 20″ x 24″.** Packages exceeding this size will be returned without panel review. Avoid using crates. Framed photographs will not be accepted.

All slides should be 35mm (suitable for carrousel projection) and must be placed in a 9″ x 11″ clear plastic sheet for safe handling and easy return. Arrangement of slides must be as follows:

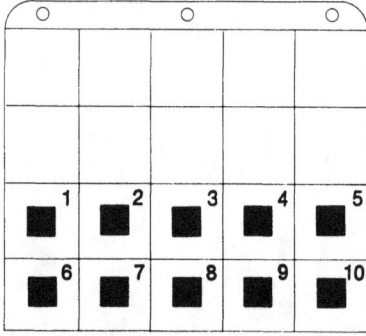

Do not submit glass slides.
Please indicate on each slide:
name of photographer;
title of work;
date of work;
top of the work;
dimension in inches (height preceding width preceding depth).

The application may be supplemented with not more than two catalogues of recent exhibitions and/or not more than three reviews of recent work. Supplementary material must be submitted with your application.

Although fellowships are not made for specific projects but to buy time and materials, you may indicate to the panel specific plans or projects on a single (8½″ x 11″) sheet attached to your application.

Applications which are not accompanied by slides or photographs are considered incomplete and will not be reviewed.

Individual Grant Application
National Endowment for the Arts   Visual Arts Program

Fellowship Applications must be submitted in triplicate and mailed   Category under which support is requested:
to the Grants Office (Mail Stop 701) National Endowment for the
Arts, Washington, D.C. 20506

| Name (last, first, middle initial) | U.S. Citizenship |
| | Yes   No   Visa Number |

| Present mailing address/phone | Professional field or discipline |
| | Birth Date   Place of Birth |

Permanent mailing address/phone	Period of support requested
	Starting
	month day year
	Ending
	month day year

Career summary or background

Amount requested from National Endowment for the Arts $_____

Education

Name of institution	Major area of study	Inclusive dates	Degree

Fellowships or grants previously awarded

Name of award	Area of study	Inclusive dates	Amount

Prizes/Honors received	Membership Professional Societies

Present employment

Employer	Position/Occupation	Total income last calendar year

I certify that the foregoing statements are true and complete to the best of my knowledge. Should a grant result from my application, grant funds will be used to advance my career in a fashion consistent with my previous performance as shown by my slides and other supportive material.

Signature of applicant ————————————————————— Date —————————

Statement of Work Plan for SUBURBIA

This project will be to record, by means of a photographic survey, the new suburban culture. My particular emphasis will not be on the traditional suburbs that surround major urban centers, but the new suburbia of the "instantly" developed tract communities. These tracts are dramatically transforming the smaller traditional rural towns into affluent, urban communities (e.g., Livermore, California, 46 miles from San Francisco, has grown from 16,000 to 35,000 people in eight years).

Most research attention is presently directed toward the dramatic social problems of minorities, urban education, violence, and social breakdown. My attention will, however, be directed to the phenomenon of isolation and entrenchment of the white middle class in the tract homes of the new suburbia.

Photographs of people in the interiors of their homes will reveal the values of the middle class, because people in the privacy of their homes surround themselves with material creature comforts that reflect their values. By photographing large numbers of families in their homes, one can gain the commonplace reality of suburban living.

Statement of Work Plan for OUR KIND OF PEOPLE

My job as photographer for the Livermore Independent newspaper gives me access to all levels of community life. I have, in the last five years, photographed every type of club activity, social function, and political get-together. The success of my book Suburbia was, in part, aided by my photo-news job. The newspaper gave my the contacts in the community. I then went out and photographed where and how I pleased, and documented the suburban lifestyle.

In photographing the social behavior and rituals of fraternal, social, and civic groups for this project, I am again using the newspaper to give me access to the community. To get the proper selection and scheduling of the 130 groups that I plan to document, I have the assistance of the activities editor of the newspaper. I have, for example, twice photographed the Elks Club for the paper. On the third trip out to the Elks Club, I was on my own (with a large format camera and strobes). This time I spent three hours covering the installation of officers. A club, this one fraternal, installing its new officers is just one of the many rituals I plan to document.

I plan to photograph seven days a week for a year. This way, no group will meet at a time that I cannot photograph them. I think the documentation of these groups is important historically. There are no photographic records of social institutions such as the Rotary, Lions, 4-H, or the Elks Clubs in existence today.

Statement of Work Plan for WORKING

My job as a photographer and advertising salesman for the Livermore Independent give me access to all levels of community life.

I have, in the last seven years, photographed every type of business, club activity, social function, and political get-together. The success of my books Suburbia and Our Kind of People was directly aided by my newspaper job. The newspaper gave me a reason to be there and take photographs.

For the past year, in addition to my photographic duties, I have been an advertising salesman for the Independent. The exposure to the business community has made me aware of the vast number of ways people earn their living in our society. I plan to continue at the newspaper on a part-time basis and to photograph: white- and blue-collar workers, businessmen and businesswomen, and the traditional "mom and pop" store.

Aside from the newspaper, to help in photographing the business community (people at work), I will use the yellow pages of the phone book. I will start by photographing an accountant and end with a zipper salesman.

I plan to spend one year photographing the business community and people working.

Statement of Work Plan for LEISURE

(Proposal for second Guggenheim to aid in photographing Leisure book.)

Photographs of how American pursue the "Good Life" tell us as much about them as their homes or work. Leisure has become a major part of our lifestyle. If we measure it in dollars spent ($160 billion), it is one of our largest industries.

Here are example of "leisure" activities I plan to photograph: tennis, boating, swimming, football, archery, jogging, and bowling, to name a few. These activities draw more than 700 million participants and spectators each year as many Americans take part in a variety of sports and leisure time activities.

As a photographer I want to document our leisure time activities. And, I hope the Guggenheim Fellowship will aid me in this project.

The areas of leisure to be photographed are:

(1) Mind, body trips
(2) Land, water and air trips
(3) Sports
(4) Cars, motorcycles and boats
(5) Games and hobbies
(6) Miscellaneous

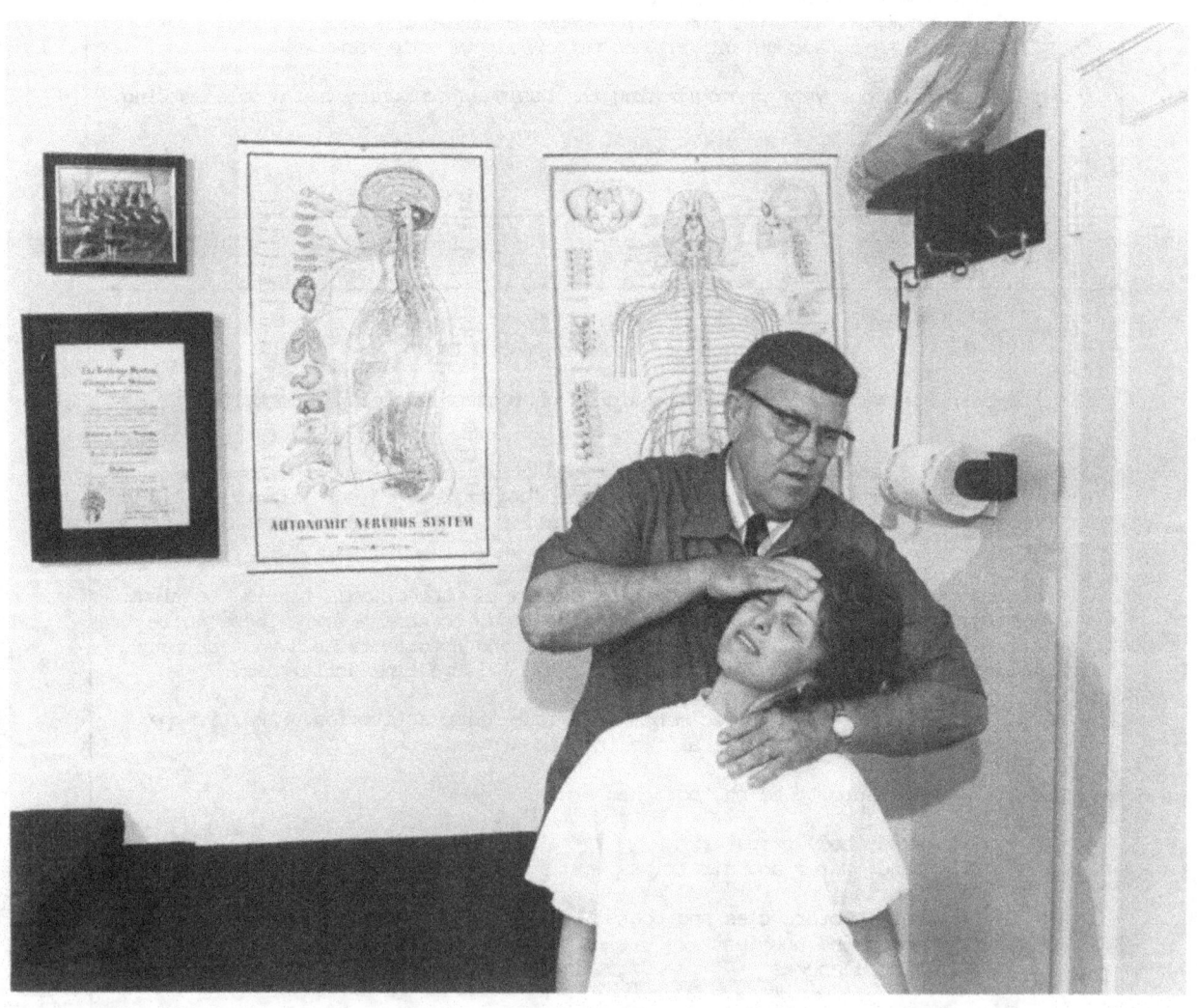

references

PHOTOGRAPHY BOOKS

A Kind of Life: Conversations in the Combat Zone, by Roswell Angier, Addison House, 1976

America & Lewis Hine: Photographs 1904 – 1940, Aperture, 1977

The Americans, by Robert Frank, Aperture (out of print)

Diane Arbus, Aperture, 1972

Circus Days, by Jill Freedman, Crown Publishers, 1975

The Concerned Photographer, edited by Cornell Capa & Bhupendira Karia. Six volumes, Grossman, 1974

Conversations With The Dead, by Danny Lyon, Holt, Rinehart & Winston, 1971

The Decisive Moment, by Henri Cartier-Bresson, Simon & Schuster, 1952

Disfarmer: The Heber Springs Portraits 1939 – 1946, by Julia Scully, Addison House, 1976

East 100th Street, by Bruce Davidson, Harvard University Press, 1970

Eastern Shore, by Steve Szabo, Addison House, 1976

Walker Evans, published by the Museum of Modern Art, NY, 1971. Distributed by New York Graphic Society.

The Family of Man, by Edward Steichen, Maco Magazine Corp., 1955

From the Picture Press, by John Szarkowski, MOMA, 1973

Gypsies, by Josef Koudelka, Aperture, 1975

History of Photography, by Beaumont Newhall, MOMA, 1964 (revised)

Dorthea Lange, MOMA, 1966. Distributed by Doubleday, Garden City, N.J.

Les Femmes, by Jacques Henri Lartigue, E.P.Dutton, 1974

Life Library of Photography, 20 volumes, Time-Life Books, NY

Looking at Photographs, by John Szarkowski, MOMA

Naked City, by Weegee, Da Capo, 1975

Photographer's Choice, edited by Kelly Wise, Addison House, 1975

Photographs & Anti-Photographs, by Elliott Erwitt, New York Graphic Society, 1972

Photography Within the Humanities, by Eugenia Parry Janis & Wendy MacNeil, Addison House, 1977

Photography Year, Time-Life Books, NY

W. Eugene Smith: His Photographs & Notes, Aperture

Paul Strand, Sixty Years of Photography, Aperture, 1976

Suburbia, by Bill Owens, Straight Arrow Books

Edward Weston, Photographer, edited by Nancy Newhall, Grossman, 1971

World of Atget, by Berenice Abbott, Horizon Press, 1975

For a catalogue listing photography books write:

Focus Gallery
2146 Union Street
San Francisco, CA 94123

The Book Bus
Visual Studies Workshop
31 Prince Street
Rochester, N.Y. 14607

Light Impressions*
P.O. Box 3012
Rochester, N.Y. 14614

*Light Impressions is a central mail-order source for fine photographic books. They often ship orders on the day they're received! In addition, for a mere $10, you can get on their Updating Service mailing list. The Updating Service will keep you informed about new books, special services and offers.

If you need an excellent photographic how-to book, I recommend the following titles:

Compact Photo Lab Index, Morgan & Morgan, 1977

The Craft of Photography, by David Vestal, Harper & Row, 1974

Handbook of Contemporary Photography, by Arnold Gassan, Handbook Company, 1974. Distributed by Light Impressions.

Production for the Graphic Designer, by James Craig, Watson-Guptill, 1974

PHOTOGRAPHIC MAGAZINES

Afterimage
31 Prince Street
Rochester, N.Y. 14607

American Photographer
271 Madison Avenue
New York, N.Y. 10016

Aperture Quarterly of Photography
Elm Street
Millerton, N.Y. 12546

Art Direction
19 W. 44th Street
New York, N.Y. 10036

Art In America
850 Third Avenue
New York, N.Y. 10022

Art News
750 Third Avenue
New York, N.Y. 10017

Arte Fotografico
Don Ramon de la Cruz, 53
Madrid 1, Spain

Artweek
120 Blair Avenue
Piedmont, CA 94611

Associated Press Newsfeatures
50 Rockefeller Plaza
New York, N.Y. 10020

British Journal of Photography
Henry Greenwood & Co., Ltd.
24 Wellington Street
London WC2E 7DH England

Camera
C.J. Bucher, Ltd.
Zurichstrasse 3
Lucerne 6000 Switzerland

Camera Canada
10 Shannon Blvd.
Scarborough, Ontario M1R LB5 Canada

Camera 35
420 Lexington Avenue
New York, N.Y. 10017

Camerart
Box 620
Tokyo 100-91 Japan

Canadian Photography/Photo Canada
481 University Avenue
Toronto, Ontario M5W 1A7 Canada

Creative Camera
19 Doughty Street
London, WC1N 2PT England

Exposure
P.O. Box 1651
FDR Post Office
New York, N.Y. 10022

Focus
Box 26, Amersfoot
Netherlands—Cor Woudstra

Foto
Box 3224
103-64 Stockholm 3, Sweden

Foto Magazine
Heering
Orttestrasse 8
8000 Munich 70, Germany

International Photographer
15 Sunset Blvd.
Los Angeles, CA 90046

Modern Photography
130 East 59th Street
New York, N.Y. 10022

News Photographer
170 West End Avenue
New York, N.Y. 10023

Petersen's Photographic
8490 Sunset Blvd.
Los Angeles, CA 90069

Popular Photography
One Park Avenue
New York, N.Y. 10016

Print Letter
P.O. Box 250
CH-8046
Zurich, Switzerland

Professional Photographer
1090 Executive Way
Des Plaines, Illinois 60018

PHOTOGRAPHIC EQUIPMENT

In addition to the sources listed below, there are probably many locally accessible (and relatively inexpensive) sources one might look into for photographic equipment. The want ads in regional newspapers and the discount camera stores listed in the back pages of *Popular Photography* are good places to start. One might also check local camera clubs for "camera swap meets."

47th Street Photo, Inc.
67 West 47th Street
New York, N.Y. 10036

Foto-Care, Ltd.
170 Fifth Avenue
New York, N.Y. 10010

Horsetrader Magazine
Box 11712
Santa Ana, CA 92611

Lens and Repro
34 West 17th Street
New York, N.Y. 10010

Olden Camera and Lens
1265 Broadway
New York, N.Y. 10001